The Birdkeepers' Guides
Macaws

tfb

Julie Mancini

Macaws

Project Team
Editor: Tom Mazorlig
Indexer: Elizabeth Walker
Series Design: Mary Ann Kahn
Design: Patricia Escabi

TFH Publications®
President/CEO: Glen S. Axelrod
Executive Vice President: Mark E. Johnson
Publisher: Christopher T. Reggio
Production Manager: Kathy Bontz

TFH Publications, Inc.®
One TFH Plaza
Third and Union Avenues
Neptune City, NJ 07753

Printed and bound in China
11 12 13 14 15   1 3 5 7 9 8 6 4 2

Library of Congress Cataloging-in-Publication Data
Mancini, Julie R. (Julie Rach)
  Macaws / Julie Mancini.
       p. cm.
  Includes index.
  ISBN 978-0-7938-1483-1 (alk. paper)
  1. Macaws. I. Title.
  SF473.M33M36 2011
  636.68656--dc23

                          2011024185

This book has been published with the intent to provide accurate and authoritative information in regard to the subject matter within. While every reasonable precaution has been taken in preparation of this book, the author and publisher expressly disclaim responsibility for any errors, omissions, or adverse effects arising from the use or application of the information contained herein. The techniques and suggestions are used at the reader's discretion and are not to be considered a substitute for veterinary care. If you suspect a medical problem consult your veterinarian.

The Leader in Responsible Animal Care for Over 50 Years!®
www.tfh.com
CENTRAL
Garden & Pet

Contents

1

Introducing Macaws

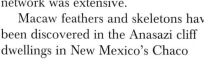

Macaws are bright, bold, beautiful large parrots from Central and South America. They have been kept as pets for centuries in their homelands, and their bright plumage attracted the attention of the sailors and explorers who visited the New World. Christopher Columbus made note in his ship's log of red chicken-sized parrots that could have been macaws when he visited the Caribbean island of Guadeloupe in 1496 (a macaw found on the island in 1667 was given the common name of the lesser Antillean macaw and the scientific name *Ara guadeloupensis*. This now-extinct bird also could have lived on the islands of Martinique and Dominica.). Hernando Cortez commented on the sizable aviaries that the Aztec ruler Montezuma II kept in his capital of Tenochtitlan.

Other early explorers commented on the brightly colored macaw feathers used by the Indians of east Brazil and the Incas of Peru. The trade in parrot feathers extended into the western United States, where archaeologists have found petroglyphs depicting macaw-like birds outside Albuquerque, New Mexico— far outside their natural range, indicating the trade network was extensive.

Macaw feathers and skeletons have been discovered in the Anasazi cliff dwellings in New Mexico's Chaco Canyon, and the group of Anasazi who lived there is even referred to as the Scarlet Macaw Clan by anthropologists. They thrived in the canyon and the surrounding desert for more than 300 years beginning in AD 829. Even today, residents of the Pueblos of the desert southwest use macaw feathers in their ceremonial headdresses. (See chapter 4 for a discussion of how you can donate molted macaw feathers for residents of the Pueblos to use in their ceremonies.)

Macaws star in bird shows at zoos and aviaries from coast to coast, and they sometimes serve as magicians' assistants, adding a splash of color to an illusionist's show.

The bare patch of skin on the face is one distinctive feature of macaws. The size and color of the patch vary by species.

They are frequently used as feathered ambassadors, posing for photos with zoo and aviary visitors at Jungle World and anchoring an eye-catching position at the entrance to the children's zoo at the San Diego Zoo in California. Macaws are also popular additions to bird specialty stores around the country.

The sheer size of a macaw is one of the first things people notice about them, but it's the macaw's personality that makes people take a second look. Macaws are far more eye-catching than a budgie or cockatiel and more boisterous than most African greys or pionus.

What Macaws Look Like

Macaws are among the largest of the parrots. They have large eyes set on the sides of their heads and a hooked beak that can appear intimidating to some potential bird owners. The color of the beak depends on the species, and it ranges from a bone white color on the scarlet to a dark grayish to black on the hyacinth.

Thanks in large part to his amazing tail feathers, a macaw's length ranges

The hyacinth macaw is the largest species of macaw and is the longest parrot species.

from 11 to 39.5 inches (28 to 100 cm). Mature birds weigh between 129 and 1695 grams, depending on the species. Pet bird weights are usually given in grams, rather than ounces, because grams provide a more precise weight measurement for veterinarians.

A healthy macaw will perch upright,

Macaws at a Glance

Common Name	Scientific Name	Length	Weight	Alternative Name(s)
Blue and gold macaw	*Ara ararauna*	33.8 inches (86 cm)	1000 to 1200 grams	Blue and yellow macaw
Green-winged macaw	*Ara chloroptera*	35.5 inches (90 cm)	1200 to 1400 grams	
Hyacinth macaw	*Anodorhynchus hyacinthinus*	39.4 inches (100cm)	1435 to 1695 grams	
Illiger's macaw	*Primolius maracana*	16.2 inches (41 cm)	265 grams	Blue-winged macaw
Military macaw	*Ara militaris*	27.5 to 29.5 inches (70 to 75 cm)	900 grams	
Red-shouldered macaw	*Diopsittaca nobilis*	11.8 inches (30 cm)	129 to 169 grams	Two sub-species exist: noble macaw and Hahn's macaw
Scarlet macaw	*Ara macao*	35.5 inches (90 cm)	900 to 1100 grams	
Severe macaw	*Ara severa*	29.25 inches (49 cm)	360 grams	Chestnut-fronted macaw
Yellow-collared macaw	*Primolius auricollis*	15.75 inches (40 cm)	250 grams	

using both feet equally to hold onto his perch. He will keep his wings snug against his body and will have smooth, shiny feathers that are free from bald spots. His long tail will follow the slope of his back and wing feathers, and its feathers will be clean and unfrayed.

Because of their large wings and aerodynamic bodies, macaws are often strong, fast flyers. They can fly 15 miles (24 km) or more in a day while foraging for food in the wild, and your pet bird has a similar need for activity and exercise. Allow your pet time out of his cage each day to flap his wings and exercise. He can play on a parrot playgym or spend time with you, learning tricks.

As parrots, macaws have feet with two toes that point forward and two toes that point backward–this toe arrangement is called *zygodactyly*. This zygodactyl foot helps a macaw grip his perch securely or climb his cage bars easily, and it also gives him a funny little waddle in his walk when he walks across the floor or a tabletop. His feet will support his weight evenly, and he will have four toes on each foot. Each toe features a slightly hooked nail that helps a macaw improve his traction on the perch.

Macaws in Nature

Macaws belong to the parrot family Psittacidae. This family includes parakeets, budgies, African greys, conures, Amazons, lories, and all of the other parrots except the cockatoos and the parrots found in New Zealand. Macaws are closely related to the other parrots of Central and South America, with their closest relatives probably being the conures of the genus *Aratinga* (for example, sun conures and red-masked conures).

Most macaws are native to Central or South America, with some now-extinct species being native to Caribbean islands. Nineteen macaw species can be found in the wild, but not all of them are commonly kept as pets. In their native habitats, macaws live in a variety of areas, ranging from swamps to savannahs to forests. They eat seeds, nuts, flowers, fruits, and other vegetable matter (along with a small number of insects, snails, and other small animals) that they find in the treetops.

Macaws are strong flyers, and in nature they often travel many miles each day searching for food. This is a pair of blue and gold macaws.

Extinct Macaws

If reports from early explorers of the New World can be believed, several Caribbean islands had resident macaw species that have since gone extinct. The islands of Guadeloupe, Martinique, Dominica, and Jamaica may have had their own macaw species, but no physical evidence remains of these birds.

Scientists have unearthed fossil evidence—a foot bone found in a fire pit—of the St. Croix macaw, and physical evidence (preserved skins in museums) exists to prove that a red Cuban macaw once inhabited that island. The last known wild Cuban macaw was shot in 1864, and the last known captive specimens died at the Berlin Zoo in the early 1900s.

More recently, Spix's macaw has been reported extinct in the wild. A lone male bird was observed in the wild in Brazil beginning in 1990, and his movements were monitored for almost a decade before he disappeared from his native range in northeastern Brazil in October 2000. A captive breeding program worldwide is underway to try to bring this species back from the brink of extinction, with about 100 birds currently in the program in five separate breeding facilities.

Some macaw species are threatened or endangered in their native lands due to a number of factors. The most obvious of these is habitat destruction. Macaws need large tracts of undisturbed land in which they can forage for food. Most species also require old, established trees in which to build their nests, but these forest lands and nesting trees are being destroyed in many parts of Central and South America. Some species were overtrapped for the pet trade before the Convention on International Trade in Endangered Species (CITES) extended protection to all species of macaws. Despite this legal protection, birds are still trapped and kept as pets.

In some cases, trappers break up family units, a practice that reduces future breeding success. If female birds are taken, fewer eggs can be laid, and if male birds are taken, fewer fertile eggs are laid, and the hens and future chicks have no one to feed them in the nest.

Another factor that contributes to the low numbers of wild macaws is the fact that most macaws are slow to mature. Since they take longer to grow up than other parrot species, they don't have as many years to breed. Once she does breed, the female macaw invests two months in incubating her clutch of eggs, but many macaw pairs concentrate their rearing efforts on the first-hatched chick and leave any subsequent chicks to starve, while other parrot species attempt to raise all their chicks. Leaving one or two chicks to starve reduces the potential macaw population, and some biologists are attempting to raise these chicks in the wild as future breeders.

Young macaws stay in the nest for about three months and are partly supported by their parents for several months after that before becoming totally independent.

Full-Size and Miniature Macaws

Macaws can be grouped into two main categories: full-sized and miniature. The macaws range from the majestic hyacinth, which measures almost 40 inches (101.5 cm) in length, to the relatively petite red-shouldered macaw, which measures about 12 inches (30.5 cm) in length.

We'll look at the five most popular full-sized macaws, followed by the four most commonly kept miniature species. (The other macaw species are rare in or absent from aviculture.) Keep in mind that these descriptors are relative—a miniature macaw still measures at least a foot in length, and most miniature macaws are closer to being two feet (61 cm) long. Even though miniature macaws are smaller than their full-sized relatives, they still require large cages and play areas to accommodate their tail plumage and wing span.

Blue and Gold Macaw

As you might expect from the name, the blue and gold macaw is a predominantly blue and yellow

bird. The birds have a small patch of green feathers on the tops of their heads, while their neck napes, backs, and wings are covered in bright blue feathers. Golden feathers cover their chests and bellies. Blue and golds have black beaks and small patches of black feathers beneath their chins. Their facial skin is bare and crisscrossed with fine black feathers.

Although their plumage is eye-catching, it's the blue and gold's personality that wins over legions of bird owners. These charming, clever

Similar to the blue and gold in appearance, the blue-throated macaw is much rarer in the pet trade and critically endangered in nature.

While the size of a green-winged macaw may seem intimidating, this macaw tends to be a calmer species well suited for a first-time owner.

birds can easily learn to say a few words or perform tricks. Be aware that screaming may be a problem with some blue and golds who are poorly socialized.

The native range for the blue and gold macaw stretches from eastern Panama through parts of Colombia, Ecuador, Venezuela, Guyana, Suriname, French Guiana, Brazil, Bolivia, and Paraguay. In the wild, blue and gold macaws eat burity palm seeds, the nuts of other palms, seeds, and fruits.

Green-Winged Macaw

A quick look might lead you to think the green-winged macaw resembles the scarlet, but a closer examination reveals several key differences in the plumage of these large macaws. The green-wing has, as you might expect, green feathers on the wings rather than the yellow ones found on the scarlet macaw. The green-wing also has a fine network of small red feathers crisscrossing the otherwise bare white skin on his face. The horn-colored upper beak is a bit larger than the scarlet's, and he has a black lower beak as well. The green-wing will also usually be the larger of the two birds.

Although his size can be intimidating, the green-wing is a fairly mellow macaw suited for novice or experienced owners. He is less likely to nip than a scarlet. The green-wing can learn to say a few words but is unlikely to become a great talker. Screaming may be a problem in some green-wings.

The green-winged macaw's native range covers a large part of South America. This macaw can be found from Panama through Colombia, Venezuela, Guyana, Suriname, French Guiana, Brazil, Bolivia, Paraguay and Argentina. Wild green-wings eat nuts, fruits, berries, seeds, and other vegetable materials found in their treetop habitat.

Hyacinth Macaw

The hyacinth is a large cobalt-blue bird with a yellow eye ring. His huge black beak is encircled by a yellow ring of bare skin on the lower jaw. His eyes are dark brown and his legs are dark gray.

Hyacinths are the largest macaws, with adults weighing between 1400 and 1600 grams (between 3 and 4 pounds). The hyacinth has a reputation for being quite gentle, despite the large size and intimidating beak. Hyacinths are recommended for experienced bird owners who can manage a large bird with a large personality.

The hyacinth's native range is the southern interior of Brazil. This species eats palm nuts, fruits, and seeds in the wild.

Military Macaw

This large, mostly green macaw appears to be in uniform, but the name is thought to derive from the fact that soldiers were among the first people to import these birds to Europe from the New World.

Military macaws are mainly olive green, with blue wing and vent feathers (the vent is just underneath the tail). Their long tail feathers are reddish on top and green underneath. The bird has a black beak, a red band of feathers across the top of the black upper beak, and a bare face patch that is crisscrossed with black feathers.

Although not as brightly colored as a blue and gold or scarlet, military macaws match their more colorful cousins in the personality department. Militaries can learn to speak a few words and to do tricks. They are usually sweet, affectionate companions that are suitable for experienced bird owners or knowledgeable novices.

The military macaw is one of the smaller of the full-sized macaws, reaching a length of 24 to 27 inches (61 to 69 cm).

Hybrid Macaws

Hybrid macaws are created when parent birds from different species are bred to create a new type of bird. Some common hybrids are the Catalina (a cross between a blue and gold and a scarlet), the harlequin (a cross between a blue and gold and a green-wing) and the shamrock (a cross between a scarlet and a military).

Hybridizing macaws is a controversial topic and has been for many years. Those against the idea argue that it pollutes some potentially small gene pools and that it rarely occurs in nature, while those in favor of the practice argue that it may actually strengthen the genetics of the birds it creates. When I worked at *Bird Talk* magazine, we took a stance against the hybridizing of macaws because of the potential harm to the captive-bred gene pool. However, hybrid macaws are widely available.

The military macaw's native range includes parts of Mexico, Colombia, Venezuela, Ecuador, Peru, Bolivia and Argentina. The wild diet includes nuts, seeds, berries, and fruits.

Scarlet Macaw

The scarlet macaw is arguably one of the best-known and easiest to recognize members of the macaw group, thanks to his appearance in many advertisements and travel brochures.

Scarlets are, as their name suggests, basically red, but they have bands of yellow, green, and blue feathers on their wings. Their faces are white and devoid of feathers, and they have horn-colored upper beaks and black lower beaks. Their long tails are red and blue.

Scarlets are among the most personable of macaws. Their outgoing nature charms both novice and experienced parrot owners. They can learn to talk and to do tricks. Biting, however, can be a problem with these parrots when they are not properly socialized.

Wild scarlet macaws can be found from southern Mexico through Guatemala, Belize, Honduras, El Salvador, Nicaragua, Costa Rica, Panama, Colombia, Peru, Venezuela, Guyana, Suriname, French Guiana, Brazil, and Bolivia. Wild scarlet macaws eat a variety of seeds, nuts, and berries. They also consume the fruit of the jocote tree, the jabillo tree, *Lecythis* trees, the Brazil nut tree, and the licuri palm.

The Miniature Macaws

Miniature macaws provide all the personality and charm of the large macaws but in slightly smaller sizes. The four species of miniature macaws most commonly kept as pets range in length from 12 to 20 inches (30.5 to 51 cm), making them better candidates for apartment and condominium living than their larger relatives.

Illiger's Macaw

Illiger's macaw is a colorful small macaw that has a band of red feathers across the bridge of the upper beak and a blending of green and blue feathers on the head and body. Illiger's has a bare face and a black beak. His lower belly feathers are bright red, and the underside of the tail feathers are yellowish-green.

Illiger's macaws are fun-loving, outgoing birds. They enjoy doing tricks and showing off for their owners. They are curious, clever creatures that enjoy chewing. Screaming can be a problem for some of them.

Wild Illiger's macaws can be found in eastern Brazil and in parts of Paraguay and Argentina. They eat seeds, fruits, berries, and nuts in the wild.

Red-Shouldered Macaw

The red-shouldered macaw, best known to pet keepers as two subspecies—Hahn's and the noble—is a small, mostly green macaw. The red-shouldered is the smallest of the

Although scarlet macaws have a reputation for being nippy, properly trained and socialized scarlets are good companions.

miniature macaws, but don't let his petite size fool you. The red-shoulder packs a lot of personality into his tiny physique, and this big-bird personality is one of the red-shoulder's most charming features.

Physically the bird is as the name advertises: he has red shoulders. The head is covered in blue and green feathers, while the body feathers are predominantly bright green. The red-shoulder has a bare face and a black beak. The underneath side of the wings and tail feature yellowish-green feathers.

The two subspecies differ slightly in their physical appearance. Noble macaws have lighter, horn-colored beaks, while Hahn's have dark gray to black beaks. Hahn's are slightly smaller and have less bare skin on their faces than nobles.

Red-shouldered macaws are very clever, animated birds. They enjoy learning tricks and may be able to talk. They are prone to chewing, however, and

Illiger's macaws are playful and active birds that enjoy learning tricks.

need to be monitored (as all macaws do) during their out-of-cage time.

The native range of the red-shouldered macaw covers Guyana, Suriname, and French Guiana, along with parts of Venezuela and eastern Brazil. Wild red-shouldered macaws eat berries, fruits, nuts, seeds, and flowers. They feed heavily on the berries of the black-sage bush, the flowers of the sandkoker or swamp immortelle tree, and the berries of the paste tree.

Severe Macaw
The severe macaw is the largest miniature macaw species. Another fairly colorful miniature macaw, the severe macaw has a band of brown feathers across the bridge of the upper beak, and the head feathers are green and blue. He has a black beak and fine black feathers that crisscross the bare face, as those of the full-sized macaws do. The bird's body is covered in green feathers, while his wings have red, green, and blue feathers on them. The severe's tail is maroon, and the vent feathers are turquoise.

The severe is a lively, affectionate little pet. He enjoys playing, is quick to learn tricks, and can learn to speak. Severes have a tendency to become "one-person birds," so it's important to socialize your pet to all family members and to encourage all family members to take part in caring for the bird.

The severe macaw's native range covers parts of Panama, Guyana, French Guiana, Suriname, Brazil, and Bolivia. Wild severes eat berries, nuts, seeds, and fruits, especially those of the andiroba and the jequitiba trees

Yellow-Collared Macaw
As with several other macaw species already described, the reason behind the yellow-collared macaw's name is fairly obvious when you first see one. This bird has a narrow band of yellow feathers that encircles the nape of the neck, breaking up the bird's green and blue head feathers from the green and blue feathers on the body. The ring becomes larger and more vividly colored as the bird matures. His tail feathers are multicolored, with bands of blue, red, and green. The yellow-collar

has a bare face and a black beak.

This is an animated bird that can be quite noisy. Some owners have found success at teaching their pets to talk in that their birds then talk instead of making less desirable noises. Most yellow-collars are playful and curious.

The yellow-collar's native range covers parts of Brazil, Bolivia, Paraguay, and Argentina. The wild diet has not been recorded.

Macaws' Pet Qualities

Macaws are highly intelligent, animated pets. Their ability to learn a variety of tricks and their outgoing personalities are among the reasons so many of them star at bird shows around the country. They require regular daily attention from their owners, secure cages, and numerous sturdy toys with which to entertain themselves when their owners aren't playing with them.

Potential Macaw Lifespans

Blue and gold: 70 years

Green-winged: 80 years

Hyacinth: 60 years

Illiger's: 40 years

Military: 60 years

Red-shouldered: 40 years

Scarlet: 70 years

Severe: 30 years

Yellow-collared: 40 years

Macaws also require vigilant supervision when out of their cages, because they are such curious, intelligent animals. Their curiosity is liable to lead them right into trouble, and their intelligence may be able to provide them with the means needed to get into mischief, rather than helping them think their way out of a predicament.

Does Sex Matter When Selecting a Pet Macaw?

Unlike some other pet parrot species, the bird's sex does not seem to matter when selecting a macaw as a pet. Male and female birds are equally well suited as pets, and neither sex shows a decided talent for talking that outshines the other.

Like many other pet parrot species, macaws are not sexually dimorphic. This means that the male and female birds look virtually identical on the outside. No noticeable changes in plumage color or body size can help a pet owner determine which birds are male and which are female.

If it's important to you to know whether your bird is male or female, ask your avian veterinarian to recommend which type of sex screening would be best for your bird: DNA screening or surgical sexing. In DNA screening, a blood sample is analyzed, while surgical sexing requires that a small incision be made in your bird's side so your veterinarian can visually inspect the internal organs to determine whether the bird is male or female.

Hahn's and noble macaws are the two subspecies of the red-shouldered macaw. The noble (left) has a cream- or horn-colored upper beak, while Hahn's (right) has a dark-colored one.

Temperament

The macaw species most commonly kept as pets range in temperament from fairly mellow to pretty excitable. Take time to visit different bird specialty stores or breeders before making your final selection so that you have a good idea of how the different species behave.

If you want a more mellow bird, consider a green-winged macaw, a military macaw, or a red-shouldered macaw. If you're looking for a bird with a middle-of-the road personality (one that's sometimes mellow, sometimes animated), think about a blue and gold macaw. If you prefer a more animated pet, look at most of the miniature macaw species or a scarlet macaw.

Talking and Tricks

While not on par with the budgie or the African grey in terms of talking ability and vocabulary, many macaws can and will learn to speak at least a few words. As noted earlier, some owners have had success at teaching their noisy macaws to talk because a talking bird is often more acceptable than a screaming one.

Learning and performing tricks is an area in which macaws really seem to shine. They are such intelligent extroverts that it's pretty easy to teach them a variety of tricks that they will usually perform for family and friends (and an occasional treat reward) without too much difficulty.

Time for Daily Care

Your macaw will require a regular daily time commitment from you. Plan to spend about half an hour preparing your pet's morning and evening meal (washing and cutting up fresh vegetables and fruits, changing the food dishes, and washing the used ones). Your macaw will also need several hours of daily out-of-cage time with you and your family. He may watch television with your family after dinner, or he may be let out of his cage when your kids come home from school.

Out-of-cage time provides your macaw with an opportunity to exercise. Even though you'll probably select the largest possible cage for your pet, he will still benefit from chances to flap his wings or climb on a playgym that isn't enclosed by cage bars.

Whatever schedule you set, be prepared to follow it daily. Your macaw won't understand if he suddenly isn't allowed out of his cage, and he may begin to scream or to pull his feathers in frustration.

Where to Get Your Bird

Macaw owners can find their new pets at bird specialty stores, private breeders, parrot rescue groups, bird marts, or through classified advertisements. Some sources are better than others for obtaining birds, so let's look at each in a bit more detail.

Bird specialty stores are frequently the best place for a bird owner to acquire a bird. Novice bird owners can learn valuable information from the store's staff, and the store can be a one-stop shopping experience, providing not only the bird but also

Also known as the chestnut-fronted macaw, the severe macaw averages about 18 inches (46 cm) long.

Do Macaws Make Good Pets for Kids?

Under the best of circumstances, a macaw should be a family pet rather than a pet for a specific child. While your child may think that he or she is ready to handle the daily maintenance of a macaw, the novelty of pet care will probably fade quickly, and the bird will remain, still needing his daily care.

Set up your macaw's cage in your family room or another central location in your home. By having your bird in a central location in your home, he will be part of regular family activities, and the central location will also help you remember to take care of your bird each day. A bird that ends up being placed in a child's room may become isolated from other family members, and daily maintenance may be neglected because the bird and his cage is not in the midst of the regular family living area.

If you make the macaw a family pet, you're helping your child learn responsibility. You can have your children accompany you to the pet store to select toys, perches, and other accessories that your bird will wear out, or they can help you select healthful produce for your macaw at the grocery store.

As your children grow, they can help with cage cleaning, bird training, grooming, or other routine care tasks as their interests and maturity level dictate. Along the way, you will be there to support both your children and your macaw, which will help your children see what it takes to care for a pet, and you will all grow from the experience.

all the accessories needed to properly care for him. More experienced owners can share bird-keeping stories with the staff and enjoy the companionship of fellow bird owners as they shop for supplies.

When choosing a bird specialty store from which to purchase your bird, take note of the cleanliness of the store. Clean stores are more likely to have healthy birds than unclean stores and, let's face it, clean stores are more pleasant to return to than those that are lax in their housekeeping.

Another factor to notice when choosing a bird store is the interest level of the staff. Were you greeted when you entered the store? Are staff members open to answering your questions and providing suggestions on food, treats, and toys? Bird store staff members are usually enthusiastic bird owners themselves and willing to share what they know with novice owners.

Private breeders are another good resource when purchasing a pet parrot. Breeders sell birds either on a small scale directly to the public or in larger quantities to bird specialty stores, who turn around and sell them to the public. Along with the young birds, breeders may occasionally offer adult birds for sale. Although such birds may be at the end of their useful breeding life, they may still have many years ahead of them as pet companions.

Parrot rescue groups may also provide suitable adult birds that need a second chance in a pet home. These voluntary organizations provide temporary foster homes for birds whose owners can no longer keep them while trying to find permanent placements for the birds. Some groups require potential owners to attend bird-owner orientation sessions or classes, while others may require character references or other screening processes to help determine which birds will fit best with which new owners.

Bird marts may or may not be good places to purchase a macaw. These one- or two-day events usually take place at a fairground or convention center and give small-scale breeders the chance to show off their birds and vendors to sell their products. Although many marts offer on-site veterinary exams for birds purchased at the mart, little recourse exists for buyers whose birds develop health problems after the event.

Bird marts are useful for potential bird owners in that they offer an opportunity to see a wide variety of different bird species and to ask questions of the breeders who have birds for sale, rather than actually purchasing a bird. Visit a bird mart and collect business cards from the breeders who sell species that interest you, and then contact the breeders for private visits after the mart has concluded.

Classified advertisements are another iffy bird-buying situation. Many birds offered for sale in the local newspaper are healthy animals with good pet qualities, but some may prove unsuitable because of behavioral or health issues. Proceed cautiously when purchasing a bird through a classified ad, and ask lots of questions as to why the bird is being given up.

Yellow-collared macaws tend to be very vocal, making them good candidates for training to talk.

2

Macaw Supplies

Before you bring your macaw home, you'll need to have some basic supplies on hand to help him settle into his new life with you. These include a cage, perches, bowls, toys, a T-stand or playgym, and a travel carrier (this last item will come in handy as you bring your bird home from the breeder or bird specialty store).

Have all these items set up and ready for your bird's use before he joins your family. Your macaw will have a less stressful and more successful transition into your home if he isn't made to wait in his travel carrier while you assemble his cage.

Basic Cage Dimensions

This likely will be the largest purchase you make for your bird, both figuratively and financially. Your macaw needs a cage wide enough for him to spread and flap his wings, and the cage must also be high enough to accommodate his long tail without having the feathers break or fray in the cage grille at the bottom.

Because your bird will spend large amounts of time in his cage when you are at work or at school, buy the largest cage you can afford. In addition to your macaw, it will need to hold a few perches, some toys, and your bird's food and water bowls.

A full-size macaw will need a cage that measures at least 3 feet wide by 4 feet long by 5 feet high (1 by 1.2 by 1.5 m), while a miniature macaw will need a cage that measures at least 2 feet wide by 3 feet long by 4 feet high (0.6 by 1 by 1.2 m). Keep in mind that these are minimum dimensions–upsize your purchase as your finances and living space allow.

Choosing a Cage

When selecting a cage, evaluate the models on display at your local pet supply or bird specialty store carefully. Remember that a macaw's beak is quite powerful, so you'll have to select cages that are constructed from durable materials and feature strong welds.

How Kids Can Help Care for Your Macaw

You can involve your children in your bird's care routine in various ways. Some children may be able to entertain the bird while you clean his cage each week, while others may find helping prepare the bird's fresh foods interesting. Still others may enjoy working with the bird during his out-of-cage time, teaching the bird tricks or repeating his speech lessons. Older children can help with the actual cleaning chores.

On trips to the pet supply store, your children can help you select toys or other accessories that need replacing, and they can also help choose the appropriate fresh foods for your bird (with your assistance, of course!).

A stainless steel cage is considered the gold standard for a macaw because of its strength and durability. However, stainless steel cages can be quite expensive, so you may decide to house your pet in a cold-rolled steel cage instead. If you select such a cage, inspect all welds carefully before purchase to ensure they're durable enough to withstand a macaw's strong beak.

Wrought-iron cages with powder-coated finishes are also sturdy enough to house a macaw. Here again, check the welds for strength and the smoothness of the powder coat finish before purchasing a particular cage. If you find weakness in the welds or bubbles in the coating, your bird will likely find them, too, and his beak will soon destroy the cage and its finish.

The bars on a macaw cage should be about ¼ inch (0.6 cm) thick to ensure that your pet's strong beak doesn't break them, and they should have between ¾ and 1½ inches (2 and 4 cm) of space between them, with the goal being that a macaw should not be able to put his head between the cage

Buy the largest cage you can afford that will fit in your home—macaws are large active birds that need the room.

bars. Ask the store staff to help you determine which bar spacing is correct for your species of macaw. Smaller species will need the 3/4-inch (2-cm) bar spacing, while hyacinths and other larger macaw species should be able to use a cage with 1½-inch (4-cm) bar spacing safely. The cage you select

Can I Use an Acrylic Cage?

Bird cages are traditionally made of metal, but you may see acrylic cages in magazine advertisements, on the Internet, or at your local pet store. These cages, which first became popular in the mid-1990s, are better at containing seed hulls, loose feathers, and other debris your bird creates, which may make birdkeeping easier and more enjoyable for you.

The biggest drawback to an acrylic cage for a macaw is the lack of ventilation. These cages work because of all the solid acrylic that surrounds the bird and contains his mess. If you do choose an acrylic macaw cage, make sure that it's adequately ventilated to protect your bird from overheating. To further reduce the chance of your pet's overheating, do not set the cage up in direct sunlight.

Acrylic cages also need to have ladders set up inside them to provide climbing opportunities for your macaw. The smooth cage sides are impossible to climb on, so ladders give your bird a chance to exercise and engage in natural climbing behavior.

Lastly, these cages scratch easily. Over time the scratches become unsightly and reduce visibility into and out of the cage.

should also have some horizontal bars running through it at regular intervals so your macaw can climb the sides easily to get some daily exercise. Newer bird cages tend to have more horizontal bars—this is a good thing.

Reject any cages that have rough interior wires or weak welds. Your macaw could hurt himself by being poked by a sharp wire, and his strong beak could easily break a weak weld in the bars. Also be on the lookout for cages with decorative scrollwork on them, because some birds have been injured by getting their feet or beaks caught in the decorative pattern.

Some large parrot cages have tops that open to allow the cage to double as a playgym. You install a perch across the now-open cage top at playtime, then fold and secure the cagetop when playtime is done. This type of cage may be an option if your home and budget cannot afford both the cage and a separate free-standing playgym.

Cage Tray

On the other end of the cage, the cage tray is another key factor to consider when selecting a cage. It must slide in and out easily, and it should be separated from the main living area of the cage with a grille that keeps your bird from playing with discarded food, droppings, molted feathers, or other debris. (The grille also helps keep your macaw in his cage during daily cleanup, so it's important that the cage you select has a grille unless you plan to chase and corral your playful parrot each day.)

Another question to ask the bird specialty store staff is whether replacement trays are available. Although many cage trays are made of durable metal, some may be plastic, which is more likely to be broken over the cage's life span.

Cage Shape

Ideally, your macaw will live in a rectangular cage, which will make lining and cleaning the cage tray easier than if the tray is some unusual shape that requires extra effort on your part to line properly. Keep in mind that you may be changing your macaw's cage for 40 or 50 years, so it's probably best to keep the cage shape simple to keep tray cleanup easy. Also, rounded cages have areas where bars taper and could possibly trap your bird's wing or toe.

Doors

Another important consideration is the cage door. It should be large enough for your macaw to fit his body through easily, and you should also be able to fit your pet's food and water bowls through the door. The door should also close securely enough to keep your bird inside the cage, yet it should open easily for you from the outside. Macaws can be clever escape artists, so you may have to supplement the door lock with

a keyed or combination padlock to keep your pet secure in his cage.

How does the door open: does it go up, down, or off to one side? Some parrot owners think a drawbridge style door that opens down offers extra play space for their birds, while others favor the side-opening door. Be wary of guillotine-style doors that slide up above the door opening; they can drop unexpectedly and injure your bird.

Wheels

Be sure to select a cage that has wheels on it. Macaw cages can be quite large,

If you buy a wheeled cage, it will be easy to move the cage outside for cleaning and to let your parrot safely get some sun.

A Smooth Finish

heavy, and difficult to move if they are not on wheels. You may not think you'll be moving your bird's cage very often, but you'd be surprised. You'll need to be able to pull it away from the wall to vacuum up discarded food, molted feathers, and other odds and ends your bird drops out of his cage, or you may decide to rearrange the room in which the cage is placed. There's even a chance you'll want to bring your macaw's cage out to the patio on a nice day. A wheeled cage will make all these tasks easier.

Cage Placement

Once you have your macaw's cage home, where you assemble and set it up is important. Since a macaw cage is approximately the same width and height as some large household appliances, you probably don't want to try to move it from room to room to find its ideal location after you've assembled it.

Choose a spot that allows your bird to be part of the normal traffic flow in your home, such as in the family room, so he can feel that he's part of your

"flock." This may prove to be more of a challenge for a macaw cage since it is so large, but you will probably be able to find some space in a room that your family uses frequently.

Some areas in the home to avoid are the kitchen, bathroom, and entryway. The frequent temperature changes in the kitchen and bath, along with the potential for regular use of cleaning products, make these rooms undesirable as macaw cage locations. The entryway may end up being too busy, even for a boisterous macaw, and the potential for the cage to be knocked

Place your macaw's cage in a spot that allows him to interact with his human flock frequently.

into regularly is too great.

Set the cage up so your macaw has a solid wall behind him so that he will feel secure. Cages that are set up without a solid wall behind them can cause your bird to feel insecure because someone or something could sneak up on him from behind.

Keep your macaw's cage away from windows or patio doors. These areas can become too hot on sunny days or too drafty on cold ones.

Finally, set the cage up in a spot in your home where your bird can sleep uninterrupted for 10 or 12 hours each night. Your bird may become prone to illnesses or behavior problems if he isn't allowed to obtain a full night's sleep, and you may quickly tire of your overtired bird's nighttime vocalizations if you're trying to watch television in the family room while he yells "Good night!" or makes other noises to try to drown out the noise of your household routine.

A cage cover may solve your problems. Select a dark-colored queen- or king-size flat sheet and put it over your bird's cage when it's time for him to go to bed. The act of covering the cage is often enough of a signal for a parrot to settle down for the night, and the darker color will help block light from room lamps or home theatre systems. If the cage cover doesn't do the trick, you may need to set up a smaller sleeping cage in a quiet room for your macaw.

Cage Tray Linings

You will need some form of lining in

Many cages come with cage-top playgyms, and your macaw will enjoying having one.

the cage tray to catch droppings and food and to make cleaning easier. Safe cage liner choices include paper towels, used computer paper, black-and-white newspaper, plain newsprint, and brown kraft paper. Less-safe choices include four-color newspaper advertising inserts, ground corncobs, cat litter, and wood shavings. These last choices are unsafe because they can harm your macaw if he eats any of them, and the cobs or wood shavings create a situation in which bacteria and mold from old food or droppings can grow,

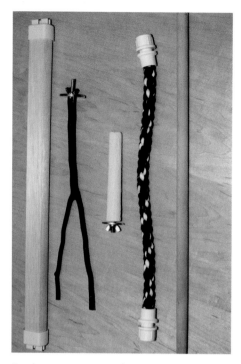

Perches come in a wide variety of materials and diameters. Provide your macaw with a few different perches to keep his feet healthy.

setting up a potential disease problem for your macaw.

Some pet stores may offer sand or gravel paper as a cage lining material. It's supposed to offer a bird the chance to consume grit, which some bird species need to help break up food as it enters their gizzards. Since many avian experts do not believe parrots require grit, the sand or gravel paper could actually cause health problems such as digestive blockages if a bird eats the paper or foot infections caused by the bird's skin being worn away by the rough paper. Use a safer, gentler cage tray liner for your macaw's health.

Providing Proper Perches

Your macaw spends most of his life standing on his feet, so it's important to provide him with safe and appropriate perches. If he doesn't have perches, your macaw will have no choice but to sit on his cage floor, and that isn't a good long-term solution. He needs to be able to sit in at least two locations inside the cage that are off the floor, which is where perches come in.

Size

The recommended perch diameter for a macaw ranges from 1 inch (2.5 cm) for a miniature macaw to 2 inches (5 cm) for a full-sized macaw. To provide adequate foot exercise for your bird, choose perches that are the proper diameter, along with perches that are either a bit larger or smaller to provide opportunities to stretch and relax his foot muscles. This helps keep his feet healthier than having him standing constantly on a perch of the same diameter at all times.

Perch Types

A look at the cage accessory aisle at your local bird specialty store shows that perches are now available in more shapes and materials than the simple traditional dowel most of us associate with bird cages. Perches are now made from rope, natural wood, concrete, terra cotta, and PVC.

Rope offers a slightly softer perch

option than wood, and some birds may also enjoy chewing on the rope. Ropes are also machine washable and dryable for easy cleaning, but they may have to be replaced more often than wooden perches because they are so chewable. Check rope perches regularly for signs of wear, and trim off any loose rope strands as soon as you see them to help protect your macaw from injury.

Natural wood perches usually provide varied diameters on the same piece of wood, which can help your macaw flex his foot muscles. Manzanita perches challenge the most persistent avian chewers, so offer your macaw a manzanita perch if he chews through other wooden perches.

Concrete or terra cotta conditioning perches can help keep a bird's nails and beak trimmed, but they may cause some birds to develop sore feet, so check your bird's feet for signs of soreness if you provide a concrete perch. Provide perches of other materials as well so that your bird doesn't spend all his time

on a rough conditioning perch. Some manufacturers offer a half-perch that provides the grooming assistance of the rougher concrete in a shorter form. This option still allows you to offer your pet an added grooming option without forcing him to perch on a full-length concrete perch for extended periods.

To get the most use out of the conditioning perch, purchase one that's slightly larger than the recommended perch diameter for your bird. That way his toenails will reach the rougher surface and are worn down. To make the most of the conditioning perch, you may find it helpful to place it in front of either your bird's food or water bowl so he'll be sure to use it several times a day.

Rope perches are suitable for macaws, but you will need to trim off any loose strands to prevent a safety hazard.

PVC perches can be almost indestructible, but they should not be the only perching surface offered to your macaw. Make sure any PVC perches you give your bird have had the surface scuffed slightly with sandpaper to improve traction on the otherwise smooth sides. Inspect these perches as part of your weekly cleaning routine and remove them if you see signs of cracking to protect your pet from the hazards of ingesting a piece of the broken perch.

One thing you won't need to purchase in the perch aisle is sandpaper perch covers. Although at first these covers may seem like a good idea to help keep your bird's toenails trimmed, they may actually harm your macaw more than they help him. The rough perch covers can cause sores on your bird's feet because the foot surface spends more time in contact with the sandpaper than the nails do. Foot sores can lead to bumblefoot and other health problems that can be easily prevented by not using the perch covers.

Placement

Place perches in your macaw's cage high enough so that his tail feathers don't drag across the floor grille. Situate a perch near his food and water bowls so he can easily reach them, and provide a secure sleeping spot that is a little higher than the other perches in the cage.

Food and Water Bowls

Your macaw will need to have access to fresh food and water while he's in his cage. Ceramic crocks work best for macaws and other large parrots They are large enough for your pet to eat out of safely and sturdy enough to withstand his daily use and abuse of them. You may want to purchase several sets of identical bowls to ensure that you'll always have a clean set when you offer your pet his latest snack or meal.

When you remove the bowls from the cage, wash them thoroughly with warm water and soap, and rinse them completely. Allow them to dry before returning them to the cage with

The varying diameter and texture of natural branch perches are good for your macaw's feet.

fresh food or water in them. Running them in a dishwasher is another good way to clean them.

Stainless steel bowls are another good option for macaws. They are practically indestructible and do not easily harbor bacteria. These bowls are often sold with locking rings that hold them in place in your bird's cage, which can help control the mess if your macaw is prone to throwing his fresh food around.

Red-fronted macaw playing with one of his toys. All macaws love toys and should always have a few in their cages.

Be sure not to place the food and water bowls directly under a perching spot in the cage, because your macaw will then likely foul the contents of the bowl with his droppings. Instead, set up the cage so that your bird can easily reach his bowls from the perches, rather than having them located over the bowls.

Safe and Fun Toys

Macaws are playful birds, and they require toys in their cages and on their playgyms to help entertain them. Toys help your bird use up some of the energy he would otherwise expend on foraging for food if he lived in the wild. Birds that don't have toys may put that energy to use in more destructive ways, such as screaming or picking out their feathers.

A visit to the toys aisle of your local bird specialty store may leave you feeling overwhelmed because there are so many choices when it comes to bird toys. If possible, take your bird with you when you go shopping so you can gauge his interest in a particular toy before you bring it home from the store.

One type of toy that your macaw may find particularly interesting is a toy that doubles as a hiding place for treats. Not only will your bird be rewarded with a snack, but he will also be challenged and entertained as he figures out how to get the treat. Many types of treat-holding toys are available, and some companies offer consumable toys with nuts, bird cookies, and other edible parts.

Homemade Bird Toys

Your macaw can benefit from some simple homemade bird toys that can supplement the ones you purchase at your pet supply store.

One of the simplest toys you can make involves creating a skewer of your pet's favorite fresh foods. You can purchase a special skewer at the store and fill it with chunks of your bird's favorite fruits and vegetables. Your bird can have the fun of removing the chunks, along with the nutrition of eating healthy foods, and you can create a completely new toy with different food offerings the next time you give it to your bird.

Another extremely simple toy to offer your macaw is a bowl of nuts in the shell. Your macaw should be able to easily crack the shells with his beak, but you may want to crack a couple of the nuts to let your pet know what's inside when you first offer them to him.

You can also create puzzles for your macaw using large nuts (the metal kind, not the edible kind, in this case) and bolts. Make sure the hardware you choose is too large for your macaw to swallow, then offer him nuts with the bolts attached. He will quickly learn to unscrew the nut, but the toy can be easily reassembled and returned to your bird. Use only stainless steel nuts and bolts to protect your pet from possible toxicity from other metals, such as zinc.

Another type of puzzle you can create for your macaw is to hide a nut or other special treat inside an empty toilet paper roll, then fold up the ends and give it your bird to enjoy. He will shred the roll to get the treat and probably then start playing with the cardboard shreds after he's had his snack.

When selecting toys for your bird, purchase only those designed for macaws or large parrots because a macaw's powerful beak can make short work of toys designed for smaller birds, and your pet could injure himself with the newly broken toy.

Examine the fasteners that attach the toy to the cage, and choose toys that feature quick-link fasteners. These C-shaped fasteners are safer for pet birds than split-ring fasteners, snap locks, or other hooks because playful birds are less likely to catch a toe or beak in a quick link.

Also be on the lookout for:
- brittle plastic toys (your macaw may shatter them with his beak and harm himself with the shrapnel);
- chains with small links (your macaw

could catch his toenail in the links and have the toy stuck onto his foot);

- jingle-type bells (your macaw can catch his toe or tongue in the small opening);
- lead-weighted toys (your macaw could crack open the toy, exposing the lead and creating a poisoning risk); and
- ring toys (your macaw could get his body stuck in the rings).

Macaws love to chew, so be sure to buy several chew toys for your bird to enjoy. You may want to purchase duplicates of toys your bird seems extremely interested in because he may go through several toys in a short period of time. Look for toys made from untreated, unpainted wood; cotton rope; or vegetable-tanned leather.

Another chewable item many macaws enjoy is a simple cuttlebone. This soft mineral supplement is the internal skeleton of the cuttlefish, and it's a good source of calcium and trace minerals for your bird. If your bird isn't a big fan of the whole cuttlebone, you can scrape off some of the bone into his fresh foods to give him a boost of minerals each day.

Inspect your bird's toys daily once he begins playing with them, and promptly replace any worn toys to protect your bird from accidental injury and also to give him maximum chewing fun!

You can supplement toys from the store with some homemade playthings, which are described in a sidebar in this chapter.

Be sure to rotate the toys in your macaw's cage regularly to prevent boredom. Change the toys as part of your weekly cage cleaning routine, and examine the toys you remove from the cage for signs of wear and tear. If they're becoming chewed through, discard them and replace them with new ones. Clean the toys thoroughly between uses or whenever they are soiled.

T-Stands and Playgyms

Your macaw will definitely benefit from regular out-of-cage time. He should have daily opportunities to stretch and flap his wings and to climb and explore

Give your macaw a variety of toys to play with and rotate new ones into the cage regularly to prevent boredom.

Provide wooden toys—or just pieces of nontoxic wood—to your macaw so he can satisfy his need to chew.

outside his cage. A playgym or T-stand will help fill some of these needs.

A simple T-stand is just that: a perch shaped like a T that features a place for food and water bowls. Some T-stands feature wheeled bases that allow an owner to roll them from room to room easily, while others are stationary.

A playgym is a bit more complicated. Playgyms can be part of a macaw's main cage, or they can be separate free-standing units. Cagetop playgyms usually feature a perch that connects the opened sides of the macaw's cagetop, while a free-standing unit can look more like a jungle gym at your local playground.

The complexity of your macaw's playgym is limited only by your budget and your imagination. If you're handy with tools, you can construct a custom playgym for your bird, or you can purchase and assemble a ready-made one.

Find an active, secure spot in your home to set up your macaw's playgym. It should be a spot that is away from hazards such as ceiling fans or open windows, and it should be in a part of your home that your family uses regularly. This will ensure that your macaw has companionship during playtime as well as supervision to keep him safe from harm.

If your macaw tries to climb off the T-stand or playgym to go exploring, gently place him back in place and praise him when he plays quietly. Don't try to restrain or chain your bird in place because he can be seriously injured if he tries to fly if he's chained or otherwise attached to the T-stand or gym. Also, being chained up seems to be emotionally distressing for parrots and can damage the bond between the two of you.

The Travel Carrier

The travel carrier may be one of the first purchases you make for your macaw because you will need something in which to bring him home from the breeder or bird store. The travel carrier will also make his trips to the veterinarian easier, and it will provide you with a temporary holding area in which you can keep your macaw when you're cleaning his cage and have no one available to watch him play on his playgym.

Your macaw's travel carrier can be a large dog crate that's been outfitted with a low traveling perch, or it can be a specially designed avian carrier. If your bird only travels to the veterinarian for regular visits, a redesigned dog carrier will be more than adequate for his traveling needs. If, however, your macaw will be taking an extended vacation in your motorhome with you, a bird-specific carrier may be a better investment so his tail feathers aren't damaged or bent as can happen in dog carrier. Your bird's needs, your budget, and your tastes will dictate the final selection.

Keeping It Clean

Providing your macaw with a clean cage is a vital part of caring for him. A clean cage is healthier, safer, and more interesting for your pet than a dirty one.

Each day, you'll need to change the food and water bowls at least once (most bird owners provide fresh food in the morning and evening and remove all fresh foods at bedtime). You'll also want to change the liner in the cage tray to remove the debris that your macaw creates as part of his daily activities.

Ideally, you should wash and disinfect your macaw's cage weekly, but a more realistic schedule is likely to be once a month, given the size of a macaw's cage. In the meantime, scrub the cage grille each week, and rinse it completely before returning it to

A free-standing playgym gives your macaw a safe place outside his cage to play and interact with his family.

Making a Macaw-Safe Home

Your macaw is a naturally curious creature, and his curiosity is part of his natural appeal. As a caring owner, you'll want to do all you can to protect your pet from harm, and a big part of protecting him starts when you take the time to bird-proof your home.

Let's go room-by-room to consider a few common things that could be harmful to your macaw's health:

Bathroom: Items to be aware of in the bath include standing water (sinks, bathtubs, and open toilet bowls), electrical cords (curling irons, hair dryers, makeup mirrors) and cleaning products (cleanser, bleach, toilet bowl additives). Cosmetics and hair care products may also harm your bird's health if you apply them when he's in the room.

Kitchen: This room is a naturally attractive place for your macaw—it's where the food comes from! Consider hot stovetops, standing water in the kitchen sink, and open ovens or refrigerators. Also be aware of potentially hazardous foods, such as avocado, chocolate, or rhubarb (for more details on unsafe foods, see Chapter 3).

Nonstick cookware can be another potential hazard to a macaw's health. The chemical that makes food less likely to stick to the cookware is called PTFE, and if it's overheated, it gives off a poisonous gas that can kill pet birds. Consider donating your nonstick cookware to charity and purchasing stainless steel pots and pans and some vegetable cooking spray instead.

Living/Family Room: The living room will quickly become your macaw's hangout, so your bird won't miss out on any of the family fun! Monitor your bird's activities in these rooms so that he doesn't try to hide under a pillow or cushion or chew on remote controls or electrical cords on home electronics. Clean off the coffee table before your macaw comes out of his cage so that you don't have to anxiously watch your knickknacks while he's enjoying your company.

Regardless of the room in which your bird plays, you need to monitor his activities carefully. Prevent the possibility of your bird's chewing on electrical cords and stereo wires by concealing them in cord containers or PVC pipes. Secure any craft or sewing projects to protect your macaw from hurting himself on needles, paints, or glues—even better to keep these items in a room or garage away from your parrot. Turn off ceiling fans and secure window screens before your bird comes out of his cage so he isn't injured by the fan blades or escapes through an open window after being startled.

By adding a sturdy perch, you can turn a large dog carrier into a suitable travel carrier for your macaw. When it's time to travel, add a towel, some toys, and some treats and you and your macaw will be ready to go.

the cage. Clean off any stuck-on food from perches and cage bars as part of your weekly routine (or as you see them), and check perches and toys for signs of wear. Replace worn or broken accessories with new ones.

Before cleaning your macaw's cage each month, remove your bird and all his cage furnishings. Put your bird on his playgym if he can be supervised, or place him in his travel carrier if you're home alone.

If possible, put your macaw's empty cage in the shower and set the water temperature to hot. The water temperature and shower spray will help loosen any stuck-on food that didn't come off when you clean the cage each week. Loosen any remaining debris with a scrub brush or toothbrush, then rinse the cage with more hot water. Shut off the shower and let the cage drip-dry for a few minutes. If your cage is too large to fit in the shower, wheel it onto your patio or into your yard and wash it with a spray nozzle attached to your garden hose.

After the cage is clean, spray it with a bird-safe cage disinfectant from your bird specialty store. Read and follow instructions for proper use to ensure that the cage is effectively disinfected. Rinse the cage completely and dry it with towels, then replace the cage accessories and let your bird enjoy his newly clean home.

3

Your Macaw's Diet

Feeding a nutritious diet is one of the easiest ways to help your macaw maintain good health. Your bird will likely cooperate with your efforts to feed him, since macaws are not usually known as fussy eaters.

What Macaws Eat in the Wild

In their native habitats, macaws eat a wide variety of plant foods, including tree and grass seeds, berries, leaves, and fruits. Much of the macaw's wild diet is found in the treetop canopy, which helps keep these large parrots away from corn, rice, and other cultivated crops. Unlike many other parrot species, macaws do not frequently raid food crops at harvest

Does a Macaw Need Grit?

As a new bird owner, you may hear some discussion about the role grit plays in a bird's diet, or you may see grit offered for sale at your pet supply store. Some birds, such as chickens and turkeys, use grit in their gizzards to grind their food, much as we use our teeth.

Most large parrot species, however, do not require grit in their diets, and offering grit to your macaw may actually harm his health because he could eat too much of it and cause his crop to become impacted. Crop impactions often require surgery to resolve successfully. So skip the grit.

Macaws eat a wide range of nuts, seeds, fruits, flowers, and leaves in nature.

time, which has undoubtedly helped preserve some species from persecution by farmers. Macaws forage throughout the day, visiting different trees in search of tasty morsels. At night they return to their roosting hole to begin the process anew the next day.

Certain species such as the hyacinth concentrate on a few food items each day, while others such as the scarlet have been seen eating 40 to 50 different foods during the day. The hyacinth also takes a novel approach to food gathering. Instead of harvesting the nuts of the *Attalea* palms directly, the macaws follow cattle herds and pick the palm nuts out of the cattle droppings, consuming the nuts after the tough outer coating has been partially dissolved by the cows' digestive systems.

Researchers at Tambopata Research Center in southeastern Peru have been gaining insights into the diet of wild macaws since the facility opened in 1990. Conservationist Charles Munn has studied the habits of the local macaws, especially those behaviors that focus on a mineral lick, which is a naturally occurring area that is rich in minerals parrots and other animals need to maintain their health. Over time, researchers have learned that the macaws and other bird species as well as other animals visit the mineral lick to obtain sodium and other dietary components that they lack. The birds also use the mineral lick as an avian antacid of sorts, helping to neutralize the toxins found in some of the plants they eat.

The Benefits of a Varied Diet

In order to maintain good health, your macaw needs to eat a diet that includes a variety of nutrients, such as proteins, carbohydrates, fats, vitamins, and minerals. While this may sound somewhat complicated, it's really pretty easy once you know what's in the foods your bird commonly eats.

Proteins, which are found in beans, nuts, tofu, water-packed tuna, unsweetened yogurt, cheeses, and well-cooked eggs and meats, provide the building blocks your macaw's body needs to grow and stay healthy.

Carbohydrates, which are found in vegetables, cereals, and fruits, give your macaw's body the energy it needs to keep going. They also help your bird's brain to work properly.

Fats, which are found in nuts, seeds, and dairy products, help your macaw's body store energy, and they also provide protection against cold temperatures.

According to avian veterinarians, macaws require 13 vitamins and 12 minerals to maintain good health. The vitamins are: A, B1, B12, B2,

Your macaw needs as much variety in his diet as you can give him.

Feeding your macaw some birdseed is fine, but don't overdo it.

B6, biotin, choline, D, E, folic acid, K, niacin, and pantothenic acid. The minerals are: calcium, chlorine, copper, iodine, iron, magnesium, manganese, phosphorus, potassium, sodium, sulfur, and zinc. Dietary mineral sources can include pumpkin seeds, carrots, bananas, nuts, and peanuts. You can also provide mineral supplements in the form of a chewable mineral block in your pet's cage.

Think of the food pyramid we all studied in school. The foundation of the pyramid is carbohydrates, followed by vegetables and fruits, meats and dairy, then fats and sugars. Your macaw can benefit from a similar pyramid with a diet that's made up of about 50 percent grains and legumes; 45 percent dark green or dark orange vegetables and fruits; 5 percent meats, eggs, and dairy; and occasional treats, such as sprouted seeds, which we'll discuss below. He lacks the necessary enzymes to digest large amounts of milk-based products, so limit the amount of dairy products, such as cheese, yogurt, or cottage cheese, you give your macaw, and cook any meat or eggs you give him completely to reduce the chances of food poisoning.

Where Do Seeds Fit in a Macaw's Diet?

For years pet birds subsisted on a diet comprising only seeds and water. Some of them lived a long time on this bare-bones diet, but many did not. Seeds play a part in the overall menu plan of your macaw, but they should not be the sole diet for him, because they lack certain vital nutrients, are very high in fat, and also aren't very interesting to your bird. Your macaw is an intelligent animal that needs a variety of foods offered to him daily so he can play with some as he eats them, and he can eat a more balanced diet instead of just seeds.

Sprouted Seeds

Although seeds shouldn't be the mainstay of your macaw's diet, they can be used as a tasty garnish to his daily meals, especially if they are served as sprouts. Sprouted seeds provide a variety of nutrients, including vitamins A, B, C, and E, as well as digestible enzymes, in an appealing, easy-to-consume format that most birds relish.

In the past, bird owners used to sprout seeds for the birds as a way to test the freshness of a batch of bird seed. Now they can be used as a healthful addition to your macaw's diet. It's best to use organic seeds intended for human consumption. Never use seeds intended for gardening, because these seeds are often treated with fungicides and other chemicals.

Sprouted seeds are a tasty treat, and they are fairly simple to create. You'll need a jar in which to sprout the seeds and some fresh birdseed. If you don't want to purchase birdseed, look for a seed mix featuring sunflower, radish, and/or mung seeds at your local health food store.

To start the sprouting process, wash and soak the seeds. Store them in a warm place to get the sprouts started. Rinse the seeds daily to ensure that they don't spoil. In two or three days, the seeds should sprout, and they can be offered to your macaw. Store sprouted seeds in the refrigerator, but, to ensure your bird's continued good health, don't hold them for more than two days.

Providing a Formulated Diet

As pet bird keeping became more popular in the 1970s and 1980s, bird food manufacturers began to examine diet options other than the seed-and-water-only diet that used to be used for our feathered pets. One of the biggest developments to result from this research was the formulated bird diet.

You can share most healthful people-foods with your macaw.

Formulated avian diets became very popular with American bird keepers in the 1980s. They were developed to provide balanced nutrition for the birds and an easier, less messy way for owners to feed their pets. Formulated diets combined various nutrients into a single food source, which reduced the chances that a bird could pick through his seed bowl and consume only his favorites.

Types of Formulated Diets

Two types of formulated diet are commonly available: the extruded diet, which consists of pasteurized and shaped food (similar to kids' breakfast cereals), and the pelleted diet, which consists of a single-shaped pellet that is steam-cooked and shaped.

Bird food manufacturers have created various life-stage formulated diets with varying levels of protein, fats, and minerals that correlate to the different stages of a pet bird's life. That is why you'll usually see growth, maintenance, and breeding varieties of the many popular formulated diets at your local pet supply store. You can also find species-specific diets designed to meet the unique nutritional needs of macaws.

Feed More Than Just Pellets

Although formulated diets are often marketed as "complete avian nutrition," offer them to your macaw with a side order of fresh fruits and vegetables. The variety of food choices gives your bird a more interesting meal than feeding just the formulated diet, and the choices also give him a chance to forage a bit at mealtime as he might if he were a wild bird. Additionally, by giving your macaw a wide variety of foods besides the pellets, you will cover any nutritional gaps these "complete" diets might have.

How to Read a Bird Food Label

When visiting the bird food aisle of your local pet supply store, you'll be presented with a wide variety of labels. The one that's the most eye-catching is called the principal display label, and it provides information about the

Healthy Food Toys

Certain vegetables and fruits offer both nutrition and play value for your macaw. These include:

- Corn on the cob
- Grape halves (leave the seeds in)
- Mangoes with pits
- Nuts in the shell
- Papaya or pomegranate wedges
- Peas in the pod

You can also use the presentation of food to make it more interesting for your macaw. Try skewering a variety of items on a hanging kabob, tucking leafy greens into the cage bars, and putting nuts or other items into crumpled newspaper.

manufacturer, the brand of food in the container, and the ingredients in the food.

A less attractive, but more important, label is found on the back of the bird food package. It's the information panel that gives you details on the food's guaranteed analysis, along with feeding instructions and a complete ingredient list.

The guaranteed analysis provides information about the minimum crude protein and fat levels in the food. Crude protein refers to the total protein content found in the food, and the useful protein level for your bird depends on the quality of the food's ingredients.

Most bird food sold in pet supply stores has protein levels that range between 12.5 and 16 percent, while the fat levels range between 4 and 6 percent. The protein levels differ between growth, maintenance, and breeding diet formulations, so select the food that best suits your bird's life stage to ensure he's receiving proper amounts of vital nutrients. The

guaranteed analysis also provides the food's maximum fiber and moisture levels. Most pet bird foods have fiber levels between 2.5 and 11 percent and moisture content of about 10 percent. Since avian nutrition continues to be a developing science, discuss your bird's fiber requirements with your veterinarian to ensure that you select a diet that is the best nutritional option for your macaw.

The ingredient list includes information on the items used to make the bird food, such as grains, fruits, vegetables, vitamins, minerals, and preservatives (if used). Try to find a diet that contains natural ingredients and limits the use of artificial preservatives to help maintain your macaw's health.

Some bird food manufacturers have developed organic diets for macaws and other pet parrots, and you may be able to purchase these diets at your local pet supply store or online. The manufacturer's name and address, along with a customer service e-mail or phone number, should also be

Fruits and vegetables should make up a large percentage of your macaw's diet.

Introducing New Foods to a Finicky Eater

If you have adopted an older macaw that doesn't eat a balanced diet, you will have to work with him each day for a few weeks to try to improve his eating habits. You can begin introducing fruits and vegetables by giving him some foods that most parrots enjoy, such as apple slices, grapes, and corn. Give your macaw a peeled quartered apple that you've dipped in seeds, or offer him a halved grape with the seed still in place, or a corn-on-the-cob wheel. Even though these vegetables and fruit aren't as healthful for your macaw as the dark green and dark orange vegetables and fruits are, these foods serve as an introduction to the world of healthier eating for a particular parrot.

To make moving to your home easier on your new macaw, feed him a diet that's as close to the diet he ate in his former home. If he has eaten a seed-based diet and is reluctant to try pellets, you will have to bring some acting skills to the forefront and act as if the pellets are the greatest snack you've ever eaten. If you can bring an overly dramatic level of interest to the pellets, this will help your macaw's natural curiosity overcome his reluctance to try the new food.

If another bird in your home is an enthusiastic pellet consumer, move that bird's cage close to your new macaw's home (provided your new macaw has passed quarantine, that is). After watching the pellet eater go through a few meals, your new macaw will be playing "follow the leader" right to the food bowl.

If all else fails, roll an apple slice or other "acceptable" treat in pellets and offer this decorated piece of produce to your pet.

In time you can start sneaking healthier foods into your new macaw's diet while reducing the amount of his former diet. Start with three-quarters former diet to one-quarter new diet, and work toward a menu that is one-quarter former diet and three-quarters new diet within about six weeks. A variety of familiar and new foods helps ensure that your new bird is eating as he settles into life in your home.

Don't quit the former diet abruptly, though, because trying to starve a bird into eating new foods doesn't work and harms the bird's health. Just keep offering new foods, and be sure to lavish praise on your new pet when you see he's tried new foods!

Are Canned or Frozen Veggies Okay?

Although some birds will eat canned or frozen vegetables, many birds will not. They don't seem to enjoy the softer texture as much as the firm, fresh versions, and the salt content in some canned foods may be too high for your macaw's health. Use canned or frozen vegetables in an emergency, but opt for fresh vegetables and fruits for your macaw whenever possible.

available on the information panel to provide you with a way to receive answers to any additional questions you may have.

The Importance of Fruits and Vegetables

Fruits and vegetables are important additions to your macaw's diet because they provide important vitamins and minerals your bird needs. Vegetables also provide carbohydrates, and fruits offer quick energy in the form of natural sugars. Served properly, fruits and vegetables also offer macaws an opportunity to play with the food chunks during mealtime or work to eat them by taking corn kernels off the cob, removing peas from a pod, or pulling seeds from a papaya slice or pomegranate section.

One of the most important vitamins found in dark orange and dark green fruits and vegetables is vitamin A, which helps build up a bird's immune system and keeps his eyes, skin, and feathers healthy. Vitamin-A-rich fruits and vegetables include sweet potatoes, broccoli, dried red peppers, dandelion greens, spinach, carrots, papaya, apricots, and cantaloupe.

When providing vegetables and fruits to your macaw, try to offer about five times more vegetables than fruits. You can feed your bird almost any fruit or vegetable, but stay away from light green lettuces, which have little nutritional value, as well as avocado, rhubarb, and onions, which can poison pet birds. The darker the green or orange color, the higher the concentration of vitamin A, so offer broccoli, Brussels sprouts, carrots, sweet potatoes, winter squashes, and/or pumpkin.

Serve fresh, unblemished vegetables and fruits to your bird, and remove fresh foods after about four hours to protect your bird from possible illness caused by eating spoiled food. Unless you know that the seeds of a given fruit are edible, remove all seeds and pits. The seeds of apples and the pits of cherries, peaches, nectarines, and plums are toxic.

Most parrots enjoy eating fresh vegetables and fruits raw. Wash the produce with some dishwashing soap and water, then rinse thoroughly and dry with paper towels before serving it to your bird. This helps remove dust, dirt, and any bacteria on the produce.

Another way to ensure that your bird isn't exposed to additional pesticides is to feed only organic produce. Organic foods are made without using artificial colors, artificial flavors, or preservatives. They are made from pesticide-free ingredients that are grown without the use of chemical fertilizers.

You can find organic produce at many grocery stores and farmers' markets. Several major bird food manufacturers also offer organic bird diets, which may be available at your pet supply store. If you have the space, growing vegetables yourself ensures that your bird—and your whole family—will have the freshest organic produce possible.

Your bird may also appreciate having his vegetables steamed or microwaved. Allow the vegetables to cool before giving them to your macaw so your bird isn't burned by his meal. For some vegetables—sweet potatoes,

for example—lightly cooking them makes the nutrients easier for your macaw's body to absorb.

Macaws Are Nuts Over Nuts

Macaws have slightly higher fat and carbohydrate requirements than other pet parrot species. As a result, they can enjoy a wide variety of nuts, including almonds, Brazil nuts, filberts, macadamias, pecans, and walnuts, as treats. Offer the nuts in their shells whenever possible to give your bird an opportunity to exercise and play a little to receive his treat.

Although technically not nuts, peanuts can make entertaining macaw treats. If you offer your pet peanuts in the shell, make sure the shells are clean and the peanuts are free from mold because your bird can become ill from eating peanuts that are contaminated with *Aspergillus* mold. Some parrot owners believe it is safer to only offered shelled peanuts.

How Your Child Can Help Feed Your Macaw

Your children can be involved in the selection and preparation of the foods you serve your macaw. Children of all ages can help pick healthy fresh vegetables and fruits for your macaw at the supermarket. With adult assistance, they can also wash the produce before it is served to the bird. Children of all ages can also help select your pet's formulated food and food-based treats at the pet store.

Older children (age 10 and up) can change food and water dishes in the cage during morning and evening feedings. Teenage children can help prepare and serve the macaw's fresh foods. Feeding macaws can be fun for the whole family!

Home-Cooked Treats

Some macaw owners may want to occasionally treat their birds to a home-cooked meal. Some bird food makers offer specially packaged soak-and-cook diets that are composed of beans, rice, pasta, and dried fruits and vegetables. These warm foods are quite popular with some birds, while others are less enthusiastic about them.

Another treat that many macaws enjoy is birdie bread. For this treat, you can enhance a box mix of cornbread with some of your bird's favorite vegetables, nuts, or seeds. If the mix calls for the addition of an egg, you can even put the crushed eggshell into the mix to boost the bread's calcium levels. Bake as directed and serve to your macaw after it's cooled a bit.

Sharing Food with Your Macaw

It won't take long for your macaw to notice what you're eating at mealtime, so be ready to share healthful people food with your pet. Your bird may even come to expect to share mealtime with you because flock members often eat together in the wild. Shared mealtime helps your macaw receive both nutrition and social interaction. Many bird owners have a portable perch or T-stand that they set up in the dining room so their pets can join the rest of the family at mealtime.

Healthful foods that you can share with your macaw include fresh vegetables or fruits, pastas (with or without tomato sauce; whole grain is best), unsweetened breakfast cereals

Nuts provide macaws with protein, fats, and minerals, and macaws enjoy cracking open the shells.

or oatmeal, plain waffles or pancakes, unbuttered toast, rice and other grains, and unsalted snack foods such as crackers, nuts, pretzels, or popcorn (hold the butter on the popcorn, too). With but a few exceptions, such as avocados, if a food is good for you, it's good for your macaw.

Other macaw-friendly foods include small portions of well-cooked meat or poultry, tofu, scrambled eggs, and dairy products. As noted earlier, your macaw cannot digest large amounts of milk products, so limit his access to cheese and milk to keep his digestive system healthy.

Now that you know what foods you can share with your macaw, here's what you *shouldn't* do: give him a bite of anything you've just had in your mouth. Our saliva contains bacteria that are perfectly normal for us but potentially very harmful to your macaw. By the same token, bacteria in your bird's digestive system are normal for him but potentially harmful to us. Sharing is good, but everyone should have his or her separate portion to eat. To further protect your macaw from the bacteria in your mouth, don't kiss him on his beak or allow him to pick at or preen your lips or teeth.

How Often to Feed Your Macaw

Most pet macaws eat twice a day. Give your bird a fresh bowl of his formulated diet, supplemented with some fresh fruits and vegetables, and a clean bowl of water in the morning. Remove the fresh foods after about two hours to prevent your macaw from eating spoiled food. If possible, give your bird additional fresh foods around lunchtime.

Give another tray of fresh foods to your macaw in the late afternoon. Refill or replace his formulated diet bowl. Freshen his water bowl, too, before bedtime, and remove the fresh foods before bedtime.

After you've established a feeding schedule for your bird, maintain it as closely as you can, even on weekends and holidays.

The Importance of Water

Fresh clean water is just as important to maintaining your macaw's health as his nutritious varied diet is. Your macaw needs water to digest his food properly so he can stay healthy. Regular water consumption helps move nutrients through your pet's body, and it also helps flush waste from his system.

Some macaws may view their water bowls as an additional bathing opportunity, but most will readily drink from their bowls throughout the day. In addition to fresh, nutritious food, your macaw needs to have access to clean fresh water at all times. Although he'll probably try to bathe in

Your macaw needs access to clean fresh water at all times, meaning you will need to change his water at least once a day.

his water bowl from time to time, he needs to be able to drink from it, too.

Give your macaw clean fresh water each day. Check the water bowl's location in your bird's cage, and move it if it's in a spot that is commonly fouled by droppings or food debris. Unclean water is an ideal breeding ground for bacteria, which can cause illness in your macaw. You may need to change the water several times a day to keep it fresh and clean.

If cage space for the water bowl is at a premium or if your macaw is a bather, consider providing drinking water to your bird in a water bottle like those used by guinea pigs or other pocket pets. During the transition period from bowl to bottle, make sure your macaw is drinking from the water bottle regularly before you remove the bowl completely. Also offer more than one water bottle to make sure that your bird has adequate drinking water in the event a tube cracks or a stopper springs a leak.

The Overweight Macaw

Although one of the most common problems avian veterinarians see is obesity in pet parrots, the good news is that most macaw species don't seem to be prone to the condition. Only one—the red-bellied—seems to have a problem with becoming overweight.

While your bird may never become overweight, it's still important to know the signs of avian obesity so you can take action if your bird starts to become fat. Signs of avian obesity

What Not to Feed Your Macaw

Although most human food is safe and healthful for your pet bird in macaw-sized portions, some foods are not recommended. These include:

- Alcohol
- Avocado
- Chocolate
- Fruit seeds and pits
- Mushrooms
- Onions
- Rhubarb
- Salty snacks (e.g., potato chips, pretzels, French fries)
- Sugary foods (e.g., candy, cookies, ice cream)
- Spoiled food

include fat buildup on the bird's upper chest or belly. A fat bird may also start to show fat deposits between the feathers on his chest, and he may change his perching stance to a wider-legged position to accommodate his larger size. He will probably be less active and may become winded easily.

A few simple steps on your part can help your macaw fight off excess weight. Give your bird daily opportunities to climb on a playgym and flap his wings outside his cage. Provide interesting toys for him to play with during his in-cage time, and give him his favorite fruits and vegetables as treats. Feed him a balanced diet and limit high-fat snacks.

4

Grooming Your Macaw

Although grooming is an important part of your macaw's daily routine, you shouldn't expect your bird to be able to handle all of his grooming needs. It's up to you to see that his wing feathers are professionally trimmed following his annual molt, and you'll also need to manicure your pet's nails from time to time and provide him with daily bathing opportunities.

Macaw owners need to be concerned with several grooming issues including bathing, nail care, beak care, wing trimming, and molting. We'll look at each area in detail and explain what you need to do to help your bird keep his feathers in tip-top shape!

While performing your grooming tasks, look for signs of grooming-related potential health problems. These can include a brittle beak, suddenly overgrown nails, or patchy feather loss. Contact your avian veterinarian's office for an appointment if you notice any of these problems with your bird's feathers, beak, and nails.

Fabulous, Fantastic Feathers

Before we delve into the various grooming chores your macaw may or may not need help with, let's stop to first consider what's he's primarily grooming: his fantastic feathers. Birds use their feathers for warmth, flight, defense, attraction, and cushioning. Scientists believe that feathers have their roots in the scales of reptiles, and the fossils of dozens of feathered

How Your Children Can Help with Macaw Grooming

Children usually enjoy working with the family pet, and yours may eagerly volunteer to help you care for your macaw. Before you involve your children in macaw grooming, though, take some time to consider their ages and their personalities, and assign tasks accordingly.

Young or excitable children can help you gather the grooming supplies before your bird comes out of his cage, but it's probably best for both them and your bird if they are elsewhere when the actual grooming takes place. Depending on the child, the youngster may be able to watch quietly, hand you supplies, or talk softly to your macaw to keep him calm.

Preteen or teenage children can help you groom your bird by acting as your grooming assistant, provided they are calm around the bird and will take direction from you without getting excited. The goal is to make grooming your bird a quick and reasonably stress-free activity, so use your best judgment as to how involved your children should be.

Your macaw will spend a lot of his time preening his feathers to keep them in top condition.

dinosaur species have been discovered since the 1990s.

A bird's feathers grow from rows of feather follicles called pterylae. The bare skin between the follicles is known as apteria. The number of feathers a bird has on his body ranges from 2,000 for a parakeet to 30,000 for an emperor penguin.

Birds have different types of feathers on different parts of their bodies. The contour feathers, which are the biggest and most colorful, cover the bird's body and wings. Coverts are found on a bird's wings and tail and cover most

of the flight surface of the bird's wing. The actual flight feathers are called remiges, and they are divided into primary and secondary flight feathers. The tail feathers are called retrices.

Other specialized feathers are the down feathers commonly seen on young birds, the semiplumes that help a bird stay warm, the filoplumes that help a bird keep other feathers in line, and the bristles that may be found around a bird's nares, mouth, or eyes.

Bird feathers take their colors from a combination of pigments. Reds, yellows, and oranges are created by carotenoids and lipochromes, while blacks, grays, and browns are made by melanin.

Preening

Preening is the part of the daily grooming routine your macaw will handle mostly on his own. A healthy macaw will devote a good part of his day to fluffing and straightening his feathers. He will preen each one that he can reach with his beak, but he may need a little help from you with the feathers on the top of his head and those on his face. Helping your macaw groom these hard-to-reach places also helps fulfill some of his social needs, because if he were in a flock of macaws, another bird would help groom those areas. Your bird will probably do most of his preening after he's taken a bath, although birds also preen their dry feathers to help keep them in condition.

You may notice your macaw seeming to nibble at the base of his tail during preening. This is where his preen gland, or

uropygial gland, is located. This gland secretes an oily substance that parrots use to help keep their feathers in condition. Hyacinth, Lear's, and Spix's macaws, however, do not have a uropygial gland to help keep their feathers conditioned.

Since your macaw does his own feather conditioning, you won't need to add any of the feather-conditioning products you may see at the pet supply store. Although these shampoos and conditioners are sold as feather-care products, many times they

Parrots cannot reach the feathers on the top of the head, so they rely on flockmates—bird or human—to preen them.

cause a bird to start picking his feathers because he wants to have his feathers clean and free of contaminants.

To keep your macaw's feathers healthy, you will need to use only clean warm water on his feathers. Spraying him gently each day with the water will encourage him to preen normally.

The Importance of Grooming

In addition to keeping your bird's feathers in condition and keeping him safe from unplanned free flight, grooming also offers other important opportunities for you to care for your bird. Regular grooming not only gives you chances to monitor your bird's health but also can also help you improve the bond with your parrot. Sound too good to be true? Let's see how grooming can help both your bird's health and the bird-owner bond.

Health Benefits

First, let's consider your bird's health. Under normal conditions, your macaw is a master of disguise when it comes to showing signs of illness. He's been programmed through years of jungle survival not to show weakness or illness. By the time most owners

Offer your macaw a chance to bathe every day. Most macaws love getting wet!

notice something isn't right with their pet, their bird is quite ill. Grooming provides you an opportunity to closely examine your macaw.

Take the time during each grooming session to review your parrot's physical condition. Does he have any new lumps or bumps, for example, or are there new bald patches between his feathers?

How do his feathers look? Are they shiny and neat, or do they have some holes or different-colored areas? A white line across the feather is a stress bar, and if you see one it may indicate an illness that requires treatment.

When you're giving your bird his pedicure, look for signs of inflammation or tenderness. Are all his nails intact? Are his foot or leg joints swollen? Let your avian veterinarian's office know if you find anything unusual in your bird's feathers or feet so the cause can be determined and treated quickly.

Emotional Benefits

Now let's look at the human-avian bond. Although many birds aren't wild about the grooming process at first, you can turn the time you spend with your bird into something special if you're willing to put in a little extra effort.

Be patient with your pet as he becomes accustomed to being groomed, and handle him gently. Encourage your assistant to be gentle and patient, too, because your bird may be able to sense if one or both or you are not comfortable with the process, which may make him more fidgety.

Talk softly to your bird as you check his feathers and nails, and praise him for behaving well. Offering a treat or two during the process won't hurt either. Pet and scratch some of his favorite tickle spots during grooming, and end with another round of tickle spot petting so he will think of grooming in a positive way. With a patient commitment from you, your bird will become accustomed to being groomed and may come to enjoy it in time.

Bathing

Most macaws are happy to take daily baths, so be sure to provide your pet with an opportunity to do so. The sheer size of most macaws makes this part of the care routine a little more challenging than with most other parrots, but it's still quite doable.

You can allow your macaw to bathe by giving him a shallow dish of lukewarm water in his cage, by misting him with clean water, or by allowing him to stand under a gentle spray of water in your shower (only when you haven't recently cleaned the shower stall with chemicals; you want to make sure that your pet doesn't get overcome by harmful fumes).

If your bird is one of those rare macaws who's reluctant to bathe, you may have to trick him into bathing by offering him some damp leafy greens. As your bird eats them, he will likely begin to play with them and may even roll around in and on them as he plays.

Whenever possible, let your macaw bathe early in the day so his feathers can dry by day's end. Wrap him in a towel for a few minutes after bathing to absorb any excess water on his feathers (and give him a few cuddles), then let him air dry. Your pet may enjoy some extra time in the sun on his portable perch while he preens and arranges his drying feathers. (Protect him from overheating by making sure he has someplace on the perch or stand where he can get out of the direct sunlight.)

Nail Care

Your macaw's nails will need to be checked regularly to keep them from becoming too long, and you will need to trim them often to keep them in good condition.

It's usually best to wrap your macaw in a towel when performing most grooming chores.

Macaw owners do not have the benefit that some other parrot owners have of having a pet with light-colored nails. Light-colored nails are sometimes easier to trim because you can see where the nail ends and where its blood and nerve supply (called the quick) begins. You may want to have the staff at your veterinarian's office show you how to manage your macaw's nails, or you may choose to have them handle nail trimming to ensure the nails are not cut too deeply.

Your macaw's nails are constantly growing, which means they can quickly become too long to be safe. Overgrown nails can curl around toward your bird's toes or get caught on his toys or cage. Either way, your bird is at risk

for injury, so you must be sure to keep his nails trimmed. When trimming your macaw's nails, remove only the hooked end of the nail. Trim your bird's nails carefully, and remove only small portions of the nail as you trim to ensure that you don't cut too deeply. It's better to cut too little than too much.

You may be able to use a guillotine-style dog nail trimmer on your macaw's nails, or you may opt to grind them with a grinding tool designed for pet care or hobbies. In either case, the goal of your macaw's pedicure is to remove only the hooked end of the nail.

For nail-trimming success, your macaw should be wrapped up in a towel. Recruit an assistant to hold your macaw while you trim (or hold your pet while your assistant trims, whichever is more comfortable for you). Catch your macaw in an old towel that's draped over your hand so that one corner is in and above your hand and the rest of the towel is below your arm and ready to be wrapped around your macaw's wings and body. Take care not to restrict the movement of his chest too much because this will leave him unable to breathe.

Hand the towel-wrapped bird to your assistant and have him or her lay the bird out on his back. Remove one foot from the towel and distract him with either a chew toy or the corner of the towel as you give him his pedicure. Clip or grind one nail at a time, and lavish praise on your bird if he's being good. Cuddle him after you've

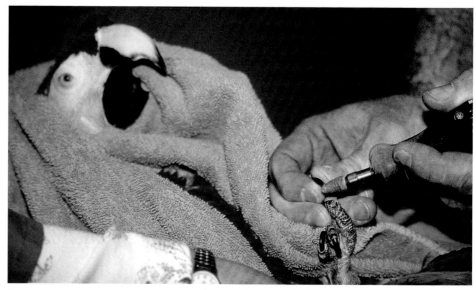

Some macaw owners use a rotary grinding tool to trim their pets' nails because the rotary tool is less likely to cause bleeding than traditional nail clippers.

finished the nail trim so he'll associate grooming with positive attention in the future. In fact, by offering your macaw treats and going slowly, you may be able to train him to allow nail trimming. See chapter 6 for basic training information, although training a macaw for nail trimming is beyond the scope of this book.

If you cut one of your bird's toenails too short, put a pinch of styptic powder, corn starch, or flour on the nail, and then apply direct pressure to control the bleeding. If the bleeding does not stop within a few minutes, call your avian veterinarian's office for more instructions.

Beak Care

Most macaw owners will never have to trim their birds' beaks. Healthy pet birds are quite capable of keeping their beaks in condition as long as they have access to a variety of safe chewable toys in their cages and on their playgyms. All you need to do is replenish the chew toys as they wear out–your bird will take care of the rest!

If your bird's beak seems suddenly overgrown, call your avian veterinarian for an appointment because an overgrown beak could indicate a health problem, such as a vitamin or nutritional deficiency or liver or kidney disease.

Since a bird's beak contains several blood vessels, it's unwise to try to trim it yourself at home. Your avian veterinarian's office has trained staff members who can handle the beak-trimming chores for you.

Wing Trimming

Wings and feathers give pet birds flight, and free-flying parrots are a beautiful sight to behold. Some bird keepers have recently begun arguing the benefits of keeping a pet bird fully flighted to help maintain its mental and physical health. Fully flighted birds have to exercise their minds and their bodies when flying and landing to ensure that the process goes smoothly, and fully flighted birds are less likely to become obese because of a sedentary, cage-based lifestyle.

Young parrots should be allowed to learn to fly and experience flight under supervised conditions before having their wings trimmed so they learn that they can fly if they need to in the future, such as if they need to escape from a predatory pet that may be trying to harm them.

Under extremely supervised conditions, allowing a bird to keep his flight feathers is a natural and normal process. Some breeding birds are actually safer with all their flight feathers because they can escape from aggressive mates. If aggression becomes a long-standing problem, however, the pair should be separated and placed with different mates.

For most pet birds, having the bird's wings trimmed is safer than allowing him the alternative of free flight. Let's discuss why your bird's wings should be trimmed annually (following his

Macaw Grooming Supplies

* Nail clippers of the appropriate size for macaws

* Nail file to smooth rough edges

* Needle-nose pliers to remove damaged blood feathers

* Old towel in which to wrap your pet

* Small but sharp scissors

* Styptic powder or cornstarch to stop bleeding nails

yearly molt, in which all his flight feathers are replaced).

A bird's wings should be trimmed routinely to keep him from flying away unexpectedly. Fully feathered birds can fly out an open door or window suddenly, even if the bird has never shown a previous interest in flying. If a fully feathered bird becomes startled or surprised, he may fly out an open window or into a wall or mirror before you even realize what's happening. Escaped birds with intact flight feathers are less likely to be reunited with their owners, too.

Having your bird's wings trimmed keeps your pet safe at home. Your bird can't become injured by the ceiling fan or take an unplanned swim in the toilet bowl if his wings are trimmed.

To be completely safe, have both of your bird's wings trimmed. Although some experts recommend trimming just one wing, having one trimmed and one untrimmed wing makes it more difficult for your bird to fly straight and level. It also defeats the purpose of a good wing trim—leaving enough flight feathers for your bird to glide safely to a stop if he flutters to the ground from his cage top while not allowing him complete free flight.

Immediately after a wing trim, you may notice a behavioral change in your bird. Your macaw may end up being a little easier to handle for a day or two. Others may become more nervous and fearful; if this is true, give your bird reassuring attention and fun distractions.

It's best to have your bird's wings trimmed by a veterinarian or professional bird groomer. An improperly performed trim can cause feather plucking and other behavioral problems. Don't perform a trim yourself until you are sure you can do it right. If you are interested in learning to do this, observe your bird groomer several times and ask any questions you may have. Because of the potential consequences of a bad trim, it's critical you are certain you can do it right before you go ahead.

Monitor the length of your macaw's feathers weekly, and remember to trim them after he molts in

addition to any time you see that the feathers are long enough to let him do more than glide to the ground. The average macaw needs his wings trimmed about four times a year.

Blood Feather First Aid

Before you groom your macaw for the first time, you need to know how to stop a feather or toenail from bleeding if it is cut too deeply.

If a blood feather is cut or broken, you must remove it to stop the bleeding. To remove the feather, grab the shaft with a pair of needle-nose pliers as close to the bird's skin as possible. Pull the feather shaft out with

Red-fronted macaw with trimmed wing feathers. Trimming your macaw's wings keeps him safer in your home and helps prevent escapes.

a smooth, sure tug. Pinch closed the skin where the shaft was and hold it for several minutes to control bleeding. If blood continues to flow, put a pinch of cornstarch on the skin and apply more direct pressure. If the bleeding continues, call your avian veterinarian's office for further instructions.

Although you may think it's painful to your bird to pull out the feather shaft, if you leave it in place the cut shaft will act as an opening for continued blood flow. Removing it offers the best way to stop the bleeding and make your bird more comfortable.

The Annual Molt

All birds molt their feathers to ensure that they have a full set of flight feathers to escape from predators and a full set of contour feathers for temperature control. Your macaw will lose his feathers at least once a year, although pet birds seem to be a bit more year-round in their molting than their wild cousins. This is probably due to air conditioning and heating messing up a parrot's natural seasonal cycles.

Your macaw's feathers will be replaced in a symmetrical pattern, and he will lose only a few feathers at a time on each side of his body. This gradual feather loss helps him escape from predators (if there were any in your home) just as he would be able to in the wild.

The old feathers are replaced by new ones that emerge through the skin in keratin sheaths. These new

Wing trimming is best left to your avian veterinarian or professional bird groomer.

feathers are often itchy as they break through the skin, so you may notice your macaw preening even more than usual. He will probably need your help to preen the new feathers on the back of his head and in other hard-to-reach areas. Gently roll the feather sheath between your fingers. If your bird shies or pulls away, the feather is too sensitive to be preened, so wait a few days before trying again. When the sheath flakes off easily and the new feather starts unrolling, you can gently squeeze the sheath or scratch it with

The Feather Distribution Project

Since 1982, a group of volunteers has provided more than 8.5 million wild turkey feathers as well as macaw and other parrot feathers to the 29 Native American Pueblos in the southwestern United States for use in their traditional religious ceremonies. The donated feathers not only meet the needs of the religious ceremonies but also help protect wild parrots because there's less of a need to capture or kill wild parrots to collect their feathers.

To donate whole or broken molted feathers from your macaw, contact project coordinator Jonathan Reyman at the Illinois State Museum Research and Collections Center, 1011 E. Ash St., Springfield, IL 62703-3500.

your fingers to free the new feather completely.

Pay attention to the length of your bird's wing feathers at molting time. As soon as his new wing feathers have grown in, get them trimmed so that he cannot fly away from you accidentally.

Your bird's personality and mood may change during molting. He may seem a bit more out of sorts than normal, or he may want to be your best friend even more because you can help him with those difficult new feathers he can't easily reach to preen.

How to Recover an Escaped Macaw

Since we've discussed the topic of wing trimming, now is an ideal time to bring up the possibility that your bird could escape one day and offer some suggestions on how you may be able to get him back. One of the most common accidents we heard about when I was the editor of *Bird Talk* was of fully flighted birds escaping through an open door or window. Owners would call or write us to express their sadness and disappointment at losing their bird, and many commented that their pet had never seemed interested in flying before. Even if your bird has never seemed very interested in flying, it doesn't mean that he won't take off if he's startled, and chances are he will quickly become lost once he's outside.

What happens to these escaped or lost birds? Some are eaten by wild predators, others join flocks of feral parrots, and still others end up miles from home because they flew frantically when they first escaped from their homes. Sometimes lost birds are found by people who adopt them, and some are turned in to veterinary clinics or animal shelters.

Here are some ways you can keep from losing your pet macaw:

1. Have his wings trimmed regularly and be sure to trim wing feathers after a molt.
2. Make sure your bird's cage is secure. The door needs to close and lock, and the cage grille needs to be fastened tightly to the cage bottom.
3. Regularly check your home's window screens, and repair any tears, holes, or loose screens promptly.
4. Close all windows and patio doors when your bird is out of his cage.
5. Never take your bird outside when he's out of his cage.

If your bird does escape, quick action on your part is your best chance of getting him back. Follow these steps:

1. Keep the bird in sight as best you can. Send a friend or family member to get a ladder in case your bird lands in a nearby tree, or have them start calling local animal shelters and veterinary offices to report that your bird is missing.
2. Play an audiotape of your bird talking, singing, or whistling to attract him back home.
3. Set up your bird's cage on your patio or in an open part of your yard. Place treats and favorite foods on the cage floor to lure your bird.
4. Use another caged bird (if you have one) to get your macaw's attention. This works best if your macaw and the other bird are friends.
5. If you aren't able to recapture your bird quickly, call local veterinary clinics and animal shelters to tell them that your bird has escaped. Provide the bird's name and a description, and leave your phone number in case someone turns in your bird.
6. Put up flyers with a photo of your bird, his name and a description. Include your phone number and offer a small reward.
7. Put the power of the Internet to work for you. Alert your local Facebook friends and post notices on sites such as Petfinder.
8. Keep hoping your bird will come home.

One way to help make sure your macaw is returned to you is to have a microchip implanted under your bird's skin. This rice-grain-sized device contains unique identification information that will allow you and your bird to be reunited if he flies away from home. Animal shelters and veterinary clinic staffs use scanners to read the chips, and staff members contact the chip registry to report a lost animal. Microchpping also allows you to prove that your macaw belongs to you in the event he is stolen. A veterinarian implants the chip through an injection, and once the procedure is over your bird won't even know it's there.

5

The Healthy Macaw

Taking care of your macaw's physical health is one of the most important parts of your role as a bird owner. Fortunately, macaws are robust birds with the potential to live long, healthy lives. However, they can still become ill. By the time any parrot shows signs of illness, he is already a very sick bird, so it's important to try to prevent illness as much as possible and treat any signs of illness promptly.

To help you maintain your bird's health and care for him when he's sick, you'll need to find a qualified avian veterinarian. Your macaw will see his doctor for an annual checkup, just as you do, and he will need to visit the doctor whenever he's sick. Additionally, your macaw may go to the veterinary clinic for grooming or boarding, depending on the additional services your clinic offers.

In addition to finding a qualified, caring veterinarian, you will serve as one of the most important members of your macaw's health care team. You are the one who sees your bird

Helping Your Child Understand the Visit to the Veterinarian

If your macaw becomes ill, your child may be anxious to be part of a visit to the veterinarian's office to find out how he or she can help the bird get well, or your child may be curious about how a well-bird checkup compares to a well-child examination at your family doctor's office. In either case, a little explanation before you go to the veterinary clinic can help your child understand what is likely to happen to your bird.

Let your child know that your macaw will be weighed, either on a perch attached to a scale or in a metal basket that sits on a scale. The bird will be handled and examined by veterinary technicians and the veterinarian.

Let your child know that there will be time for questions at the end of the examination, and let him or her come up with one or two to ask the doctor or clinic staff. Also let your child know that you will be answering some questions about the bird's appetite, his normal activities, and other aspects of his care. Perhaps your child can provide an answer or two during the examination to help him or her become comfortable talking to medical professionals.

Although they may want to help just as much as their older siblings do, it's probably not a good idea to have preschool-age or younger children attend the bird's veterinary visit. Your focus needs to be on your macaw's health, so children who accompany you need to be old enough to sit quietly and follow your instructions, and they must also be mature enough to not become upset while the bird is being examined.

daily, and you will soon know his daily routine. You'll know how much he sleeps each night, how much he eats and drinks during the day, and how he looks.

Along with monitoring your bird's daily routine, you'll be the one offering fresh food and water each day and making sure the cage is kept clean. You'll also be in charge of keeping your macaw's surroundings safe and interesting so he isn't injured accidentally or doesn't become bored and start engaging in negative behaviors like screaming, biting, or feather picking.

If you notice any changes in any aspect of his routine, you need to take your bird for an evaluation at the veterinarian's office immediately. Macaws and other pet birds instinctively hide signs of illness for as long as they can because in the wild birds that act differently from other members of the flock are usually singled out by predators. Even though your macaw no longer lives in the jungle, his survival instinct is strong, so his natural inclination is to act as normally as he can for as long as he can.

Macaws are generally healthy birds, but a conscientious owner will always be on the lookout for possible health problems.

Selecting an Avian Veterinarian

When looking for a veterinarian to treat your macaw, try to locate an avian practice specialist. These veterinarians have special interests in pet birds and have passed examinations offered by the American Board of Veterinary Practitioners that allow them to call themselves avian practice specialists. If you cannot find a specialist in your area, search for a veterinarian who is affiliated with the Association of Avian Veterinarians or who has a long-standing interest in and experience with caring for pet birds.

If you're new to the world of birds, use existing resources, such as the breeder or bird specialty store where you purchased your macaw, to locate

Take your macaw to an avian veterinarian for a checkup yearly to ensure he is healthy and to catch any health problems as early as possible.

an avian veterinarian. You may have bird-owning friends who can also recommend qualified veterinarians, or you can contact local bird clubs to request referrals.

If none of those resources is available, try searching either online or in your phone book for veterinarians. Look for display ads that mention bird care in your Yellow Pages, or search for "bird vet [your location]" on the Internet.

Once you've located a few clinics that appear to treat birds, call each one and ask some questions. Find out how many birds–especially macaws–the practice sees each week or month, and ask whether any of the clinic staff own birds. Ask how much a routine office visit costs and what forms of payment are accepted.

If you live in a part of the country where no avian veterinarians have set up practices, try to find a veterinarian in your area who at least has an interest in birds. Contact veterinarians whose practices see small animals or exotic pets, because they are more likely to be able to care for your parrot than a livestock veterinarian.

After you've made your calls, you should have located a clinic for your macaw. Set up an appointment for your bird to be evaluated, and make a list of questions or some notes about any aspect of your bird's care that you would like to discuss with the doctor or clinic staff. Take this list with you to the office. Be sure to arrive about 20 minutes early for your first appointment in order to fill out the new patient paperwork.

What to Expect at the Office Visit

Under normal circumstances, your macaw's first veterinary visit will probably be a well-bird checkup. If you are purchasing your macaw from a breeder, and he is your only pet, you will probably have a time limit established for this veterinary visit to ensure your bird's health. If you have other pet birds in your home, you will want to have your macaw's health evaluated as soon as possible to protect both the birds already in your home and your new pet.

The first clinic staff member who will evaluate your bird will probably be a veterinary technician who will weigh your macaw and ask some questions about his daily care and the reason for his appointment. The technician fills much the same role that a nurse or clinical assistant has at a physician's office, checking vital signs and making intake notes in a patient's chart.

The Physical Exam

Once your macaw has been weighed and your answers noted in his chart, the avian veterinarian will begin to examine your bird. The first part of the exam will be a visual check of your bird in his travel carrier or sitting on the exam table. The avian veterinarian will give your bird an opportunity to become acclimated to the room before any hands-on examination begins. During the visual exam the doctor may ask additional questions about your bird's care and routine, or you may have an opportunity to ask questions of the doctor.

If necessary, your vet will show you how to give your macaw medication at home.

Pet Health Insurance

One payment method you may or may not be aware of is pet bird health insurance. Similar to human health insurance, pet bird insurance helps cover the cost of routine and urgent care for your parrot, including diagnostic tests, surgeries, prescriptions, and routine care. Ask about applying for coverage at your veterinarian's office.

While conducting the hands-on examination, the veterinarian will examine your bird from head to tail, with special attention to your macaw's eyes, beak, mouth, and nares (you probably think of them as nostrils over your bird's beak). The doctor will also feel your bird's body and wings for lumps, bumps, or anything else unusual and will check your bird's skin, feet, and feathers for any signs of parasites or other problems.

Tests

At the conclusion of the hands-on exam, the doctor may recommend laboratory tests for your macaw, such as blood work, fecal screens, or X-rays. Each test helps the clinic staff monitor your bird's health, but the tests can be confusing to a bird owner. Let's look at the kind of health information each test provides.

Blood work, such as a complete blood count or a blood chemistry panel, measures levels of protein, cholesterol, creatinine, calcium, glucose, uric acid, potassium, and sodium, along with percentages of different types of blood cells. This information can help a veterinarian determine whether a bird has a specific illness and whether the internal organs are functioning normally.

Fecal screens help the veterinarian determine whether a bird has internal parasites or infections.

X-rays show the inside of your bird's body, which can help a veterinarian check for broken bones, puncture injuries, or ingested foreign objects. Tumors may also show up in an X-ray.

Finishing Up

After he or she has discussed the recommended lab tests, the veterinarian will probably ask whether you have any questions or concerns. Refer to the list of questions you made after you made the appointment, or ask follow-up questions about your bird's examination. If the doctor has recommended changes in your bird's diet or prescribed a medication, make sure you understand how you are supposed to help your macaw before you leave the exam room. Stop at the scheduling desk on your way out of the clinic to set up any additional appointments your bird may need and pay your bill.

Healthy macaws should visit the veterinarian each year for an annual checkup. If your bird has an underlying health condition or if he's fallen ill, he will need to visit the clinic more often to maintain or regain his health.

The Signs of Illness

Knowing how to tell whether your macaw is sick is a vitally important part of bird ownership. As noted earlier, all parrots are extremely good at hiding illness, so you need to learn what your bird's normal behavior looks like so you'll know immediately when something changes and when you need to call the veterinarian.

Instead of discussing symptoms as human physicians do, many veterinarians talk about clinical signs of illness. They make this differentiation because symptoms imply that a patient can tell his or her doctor about the problem, while signs are physical indicators that need no verbal explanation. Even though many parrots can and do talk, it's unlikely they'll tell their veterinarian where and when it hurts and when the problem started, so your bird's doctor has come to rely on certain physical signs as indicators of illness.

Here are some signs of illness to watch out for:
- Appetite loss
- Breathing problems
- Change in appearance (feather condition, ability to groom self)
- Change in appearance of droppings (color, consistency, ratio of solid to liquid)
- Change in elimination (going more or less often than normal)
- Consistently fluffed-up appearance
- Drooping wings
- Increase in time spent sleeping
- Lameness
- Loss of interest in toys and surroundings
- Regurgitated food appears on cage floor
- Runny eyes or nares
- Tail bobbing while breathing
- Weight loss

Emergency Care for Your Macaw

Sometimes your macaw may find himself in need of emergency medical care. Be familiar with your regular veterinarian's emergency policy. If the vet doesn't offer after-hours and emergency care, ask for referrals during your first well-bird examination visit. Make sure you have instruction on how to get to the emergency clinic from your home, along with the facility's address and telephone number, before an emergency occurs. Put this information in an easy-to-find place, such as your car's glove compartment, your day planner, or in a plastic bag attached to the handle of your bird's travel carrier so it will be immediately available when you need it. Always call ahead before bringing your bird in for emergency care. Stay calm and answer any questions the receptionists asks—this will allow the staff to prepare for the situation and offer them the best chance of helping your pet.

Here are some first-aid steps to take

to help your macaw before he's seen by a veterinarian.

Animal Bites

Clean and bandage any skin wounds, then keep your macaw warm and quiet. Have your bird evaluated within 48 hours of the bite to ensure that he doesn't go into shock, develop a bacterial infection from the bite, or have an underlying crush injury to his internal organs from the bite. If your macaw is bitten by a cat, there's a chance he could develop an infection called pasteurellosis, which is caused by bacteria (*Pasteurella multocida*) in the cat's mouth. This infection can quickly develop into a serious condition if left untreated.

Bleeding

Apply direct pressure and/or a pinch of cornstarch to control bleeding. If your macaw has broken a blood feather, pull it out with needle-nose pliers, and then apply cornstarch and direct pressure to the bird's wing. Contact your veterinarian's office for more instructions if the bleeding does not stop.

Breathing Problems

Set up a vaporizer or nebulizer or run a hot, steamy shower. Contact your veterinarian's office for further instructions.

Broken Beak

Keep the bird quiet. Try to stop bleeding with cornstarch and direct pressure. Contact your veterinarian's office for additional instructions.

Broken Bones

Keep the bird warm and quiet. Do not attempt to splint or set the break yourself, especially if a bone is sticking through your bird's skin. Take the bird to an emergency animal clinic or to your veterinarian's office for follow-up care.

Burns

Mist affected area with cool water. Do not apply butter

An increase in the amount of time your macaw spends sleeping can indicate that he's ill.

or other greasy substances to the burn. Take the bird to an emergency animal clinic or your veterinarian's office for additional treatment.

Concussion

Concussions are usually the result of a collision during flight, but they can also result from roughhousing with other pets in the home. Signs of a concussion include unconsciousness, loss of coordination, and loss of balance. Keep the bird warm and quiet. Contact your veterinarian's office for more information.

Frostbite

Frostbite is most often seen in outdoor aviary birds whose owners are unprepared for a sudden cold snap. It is rarely seen in pet birds that are kept indoors. Signs of frostbite include patches of skin that are cold and hard to the touch. Keep the bird warm and quiet. Contact your veterinarian's office for instructions on warming the frostbitten area.

Heatstroke

Put your macaw in front of a fan or stand him in a bowl of cool water to

Concussions usually are caused by a collision with a window or ceiling fan during flight.

lower his body temperature. Give him cool water to drink or drop water into his mouth with an eyedropper. Contact your veterinarian's office for more instructions.

Poisoning

Signs of poisoning can present themselves in different ways, depending on the type of poison and on whether your bird inhaled the poison, consumed it, or absorbed it through his skin. If your bird has inhaled something dangerous, get him outside into fresh air as quickly as possible. If he's consumed or absorbed something hazardous, contact your

Avian First Aid Kit

Here are some avian first-aid supplies you should have on hand:

* * Bandages
* * Cornstarch or styptic powder to control bleeding
* * Disinfectant solution, such as hydrogen peroxide or Betadine scrub
* • Energy and electrolyte supplement, such as Gatorade or Pedialyte
* • Eye dropper
* • Grooming tools (nail clippers, nail file, needle-nose pliers)
* • Heating pad or other heat source
* • Saline solution
* • Scissors with rounded tips
* • Small flashlight
* • Small towels for catching and holding your bird
* • Tweezers

avian veterinarian's office or a poison control hotline for further instructions. Stay calm but act as fast as possible.

Seizures

Seizures can result from a head injury, poison ingestion, or an underlying medical condition. Keep the bird warm and quiet. Transfer him to his travel carrier to protect him from further harm. Take him to an emergency animal clinic or your veterinarian's office for additional treatment.

Common Parrot Illnesses

Although they are robust large parrots, macaws can still contract some common diseases affecting psittacine birds that need to be diagnosed by your veterinarian in order to be treated effectively. Some of the most common are listed below in alphabetical order.

Allergies

Although your avian veterinarian may never officially diagnose allergies in your macaw, there are many indications that pet birds can and do suffer from allergies. Blue and golds seem particularly prone to allergy problems that affect the respiratory system and the sinuses. Causes may include molds, pollens, dust mites, dusty cage covers, and even certain foods.

Clinical signs include sneezing, runny nares and eyes, and possible digestive system difficulties. Medications may help alleviate some of the clinical signs, and you can also make your bird feel better by limiting his exposure to allergens, once you determine what they are.

Egg Binding

Although many people believe you need a pair of birds to create eggs, a healthy mature female bird may lay eggs without having a male bird around (in fact, this is exactly how I learned the sex of my African grey parrot). When a female bird cannot successfully lay an egg, she is said to be egg-bound. She will repeatedly try to lay the egg, but it is stuck inside her, and she may need surgery to resolve the problem completely. Several factors, including poorly shaped eggs, overbreeding, and low blood calcium levels, can cause egg binding.

If your hen is sitting on her cage floor, panting and straining as if to eliminate, she may be egg-bound. If she will let you, pick the bird up and look at her vent. A partially laid egg may be protruding from the vent.

To help your hen expel the egg, place her in a warm, humid bathroom with a hot shower running. The humidity and heat can sometimes help her successfully lay the egg. If she has not laid the egg successfully in about 10 minutes after beginning this treatment, she needs urgent care to resolve this medical emergency. Contact your veterinarian's office for further instructions on how to treat your egg-bound hen.

Feather Problems

A wide variety of clinical signs ranging from poor molting, stress bars on feathers, and feather picking can indicate a feather problem. Some blue and golds are particularly prone to feather cysts, which can require veterinary care. These cysts appear as lumps or bumps on the bird's back or chest in line with other feathers. Sometimes part of the ingrown feather can be seen beneath the bird's skin. Minor surgery is required to open the

Just like humans, macaws can suffer from allergies that cause sneezing, runny eyes, and runny nares.

Excessive scratching may indicate your macaw has a problem with his skin or feathers.

cyst and remove the ingrown feather.

If your bird doesn't seem to molt completely or if he has thin white bars across the width of his feathers or small holes in the feathers, call your veterinarian's office for an appointment. Feather problems can be indicative of underlying physical problems that your veterinarian needs to evaluate.

Gout

Some macaws may develop a form of gout when they are young. Gout develops when a bird's kidneys are unable to eliminate all the nitrogenous wastes that their bodies produce. The birds gather uric acid in their lower legs or internal organs. Gout has been reported in blue-and-gold, military, and red-shouldered macaws.

Your bird may need his diet altered to include more vegetables and fruit if he's diagnosed with gout. He may also be switched to a lower-protein diet and have medications prescribed to help remove uric acid from his system.

Infections

Macaws and other parrots can contract infections caused by bacteria, fungi, or viruses. Clinical signs can include loss of interest in daily activities, appetite loss, sneezing, lethargy, and nasal congestion. Your veterinarian will need to determine the cause of the infection in order to prescribe the correct medication to treat it.

Obesity

While it may not have been considered a disease in the past, obesity can be a contributing cause to future diseases in pet birds just as it is in people. Occasionally avian obesity is caused by a malfunctioning thyroid gland, but most pet birds become overweight by eating too much food without receiving adequate exercise to expend some of the calories they consume.

Signs of obesity in a pet macaw can include gaps in the feathers on the bird's upper chest and abdomen caused by fat buildup beneath the skin, fat deposits along the bird's flanks and across his abdomen, a decreased activity level, breathing problems, or limited movement because of underlying joint problems.

Some of the potential avian health problems associated with obesity include diabetes; heart disease; arthritis and other problems with bones and joints; thyroid disease; pancreatitis; and liver disease.

Feeding your macaw a balanced diet

Stress and Your Macaw's Health

Although stress is part of everyday life for both people and parrots, too much stress can harm your macaw's health. If you notice your bird has started shaking, screaming, pulling his feathers, or sleeping poorly, he could be feeling overly stressed, which could eventually cause him to become ill. Other signs of stress include diarrhea, a loss of appetite, and your bird's sitting up as tall as he can on his perch in such a way thae he appears thin.

Here are a few things that can increase your macaw's stress level:

- Change in daily schedule (mealtime, playtime, or bedtime becomes uncertain or less frequent)
- Change in diet
- Change in household makeup (a roommate or partner moves in or out, a new baby joins the family)
- Different cage location in home
- New cage (even if the new cage is bigger or better)
- Unclean cage

To help reduce the stress in your macaw's life, give him a predictable routine. Serve him his meals at about the same time each day and provide him with several opportunities each day to exercise and play outside his cage. Put him to bed at the same time, and make sure he's getting at least 10 hours of sleep. Keep his cage in a room in your home that's active, but not too active, so he has opportunities to rest each day. Change his cage paper daily and his food and water bowls at least once a day. Clean his cage each week, and rotate the toys in his cage after it's been cleaned.

Although macaws need more fat and protein in their diets than other parrots, overfeeding nuts, seeds, and other high-fat foods can cause obesity.

and saving nuts and other higher-fat foods as occasional treats is your best defense against creating an overweight bird. Also give your macaw ample opportunities to exercise outside his cage each day, along with a variety of interesting toys that will encourage him to exercise inside his cage.

Ask your veterinarian what your macaw's ideal weight range should be, and then invest in a kitchen scale or bird scale that weighs in grams. Monitor your bird's weight weekly to track losses and gains, especially if he's on the high end of his weight range. If your bird is obese, discuss dietary changes with your veterinarian

and implement them for your bird's health.

Polyomavirus

This virus, which has also been known as budgerigar fledgling disease, papovavirus, and French moult, interferes with the proper development of an infected bird's tail and flight feathers. Some birds do not develop feathers in these locations, while others have feathers that grow improperly.

Polyomavirus is transmitted through feather dust or droppings of an infected bird, or by direct contact with a sick bird. Some adult birds carry the disease and pass it to other birds without showing signs of illness themselves.

Clinical signs include appetite loss, bleeding under the skin, diarrhea, paralysis, regurgitation, and weakness. A vaccination is available to protect your macaw from this disease, and most breeders routinely vaccinate their baby birds to protect them from contracting polyomavirus. There is no cure for the disease once a bird catches it, but treatments are available that are extending the length and quality of an infected bird's life.

Proventricular Dilatation Disease Syndrome (PDDS)

First discovered in macaws and formerly called macaw wasting disease, PDDS is a fatal disease that affects a bird's digestive system. It can be passed from parent to chick during feeding or between birds in a flock.

PDDS-infected birds may pass whole seeds or other food items in their droppings. They also may act depressed, regurgitate frequently, be extremely weak, or have seizures. Research continues at the University of Georgia to find a cure for PDDS.

Psittacine Circovirus 1

This incurable virus was originally thought to affect only cockatoos and was first called cockatoo syndrome, then psittacine beak and feather disease syndrome or PBFDS. Researchers now know that more than 40 parrot species can catch this disease, which often shows itself through pinched or clubbed feathers. Affected birds can also have beak fractures and mouth ulcers. This highly contagious fatal disease is most common in birds less than three years of age. It is less common now in macaws and larger parrots because breeders have culled infected birds from their flocks, but it still can be found in lovebirds, lories, and lorikeets, where testing of breeding stock is less commonly

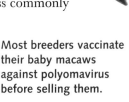

Most breeders vaccinate their baby macaws against polyomavirus before selling them.

done. Vaccine development has been underway in the United States and Australia, but a lack of funding has slowed the research projects.

Psittacosis

Also called parrot fever or ornithosis, psittacosis is a parasitic disease caused by the organism *Chlamydophyla psittaci*. Infected birds may suffer appetite and weight loss, act depressed, and pass lime-green droppings. A course of treatment including a medicated food will usually clear up the infection in your pet. Some birds can carry and spread this disease for their entire lives without ever showing signs of illness themselves.

Psittacosis is a zoonotic disease, which means it can be passed between parrots and people. If someone in your home has a compromised immune system, he or she may contract psittacosis; the chances of a healthy adult contracting psittacosis from a pet bird are quite low.

Unseen Dangers

Nonstick coatings can produce fumes that are highly toxic to birds. Although we usually think of these coatings being found on cookware, they are actually present on a plethora of household devices. Many are found in the kitchen, making this an unsafe place to station your macaw's cage. Ovens and oven racks, burner pans, waffle irons, and even bread machines can have nonstick coatings. Outside the kitchen, space heaters, hairdryers, clothes irons, and ironing board covers also frequently contain these dangerous surfaces. Remember that the fumes travel, so even if your macaw is not in the room in which you are using the item, he may be affected. To help keep your bird safe from the dangerous fumes, open a few windows or at least run a fan whenever you must use one of these devices.

Psittacosis in humans manifests itself with a cluster of flu-like symptoms, so check with your doctor if you suddenly develop the flu after bringing a pet bird home. Antibiotics are usually prescribed to treat psittacosis.

Pulmonary Hypersensitivity Syndrome

Some macaws have developed a progressive respiratory problem related to being housed in areas with inadequate ventilation or being housed with a parrots that carry more feather dust, such as cockatoos or African greys. Clinical signs include wheezing, shortness of breath, and dry cough. Affected birds should be placed in an area with good ventilation to help alleviate some of the clinical signs. Your veterinarian may also prescribe medication to help ease some of the

clinical signs of this condition.

Vitamin A Deficiency

Macaws and other pet birds need vitamin A to help keep their immune systems healthy, but some birds, especially those that eat primarily seed-based diets, do not receive enough vitamin A in their diets to maintain good health.

This problem used to be more commonplace when pet parrots were imported in great numbers, but it still should be mentioned as a reminder to bird owners about the importance of a varied diet containing vitamin A-rich fresh foods.

Clinical signs of vitamin A deficiency can include breathing difficulties, chronic infections, mouth sores, and vision problems. You can easily prevent a vitamin A deficiency in your macaw by offering him a diet full of dark green and dark orange vegetables and fruits, such as broccoli, sweet potatoes, carrots, dried or fresh red peppers, cantaloupe, papaya, and apricots.

Caring for an Older Macaw

A well-cared-for macaw can live past age 50, but he may need a little more care as he ages than he did as a young adult bird. Depending on his overall health, he may still be able to visit the veterinarian only for an annual checkup, but many older birds require more frequent veterinary visits to manage some of their chronic health conditions, especially those involving the heart, liver, or kidneys.

Veterinarian Susan Clubb, who cared for the macaws at Parrot Jungle in Florida for years, noted the following physical changes in birds after the age of 35: cataracts, change in iris color, dermatological changes, joint stiffness, reproductive changes, and loss of muscle tone.

One of the biggest adjustments to make as your macaw ages is his diet to help him fight off obesity as his activity level decreases. He should receive a diet with a lower fat level than he did as a younger bird. Ask your veterinarian's office for diet suggestions.

Because your macaw may be prone to arthritis and other joint problems as he ages, he may enjoy having a small heat lamp set up near his cage. Place the lamp so that he can sit by it when he's feeling chilly or stiff, but also leave him room to move away from it if he becomes too warm.

Prevent vitamin A deficiency by feeding your macaw plenty of orange and dark green vegetables.

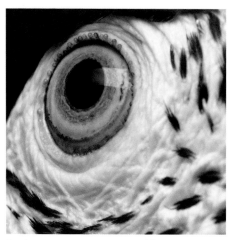
Senior macaws are susceptible to cataracts.

Cataracts are a common problem in older macaws. If left untreated, they can lead to blindness. Discuss cataract surgery with your veterinarian to see whether it is an option for your pet.

Older macaws may also have poorer feather condition, or they may lose some of the feather lines on their faces as they age. They may also develop thinning skin on their feet, and the skin color may change as well.

Pay special attention to your older macaw's appearance and routine to help detect health problems before they become serious, and notify your avian veterinarian promptly of any changes to ensure your bird has the best chance to recover from an illness in his later years.

If You Bring Home Another Bird

You've enjoyed your macaw's company so much that you want to add another bird to your home. While this seems like a great idea at first, it should be thought through carefully to ensure the physical and mental health of both birds.

If you're going to add another bird that you anticipate will be a playmate for your macaw, don't select a small parrot, because your macaw's powerful beak could easily injure a smaller bird during playtime. Even medium-size parrots are at risk from a macaw bite, so it may be best to choose another large parrot as a companion for your macaw.

Adding another bird to your home could add to your macaw's stress level, which could eventually have an impact on his physical health. Signs of stress can include shaking, screaming, feather pulling, sleep disturbances, unusual posturing on the perch, appetite loss, and diarrhea. To help reduce your macaw's stress level, he needs a predictable routine that includes regular mealtimes, regular out-of-cage play sessions, and regular cage cleanings.

If you do decide to add a bird to your flock, you'll need to follow a quarantine procedure for about 60 days to ensure the health of both your existing and new birds. House the new bird in a room separate from your macaw and in a different part of the house (if possible). Feed, water, and care for the cage of the new arrival after you've taken care of your macaw, and wash your hands thoroughly afterward to maintain your macaw's health.

Follow an equally strict cleanup routine if you visit bird specialty stores or bird marts; doing so will help to

If you want your flockmates to be as friendly with each other as these macaws are, introduce them slowly and don't force interactions.

protect the health of your feathered house members. To protect your bird's health, you should shower and change clothes before handling your birds after being around other birds that aren't kept in your home.

To protect the health and safety of your macaw and your new parrot after he's passed quarantine without showing signs of illness, introduce the birds to each other gradually, maintaining separate cages for both birds at all times. Gradually move the cages closer to one another to allow both birds time to become acquainted.

If you see no signs of stress (screaming, lunging at one another,

feather pulling), allow both birds to be out of their cages together without forcing them to be in contact with one another. Supervise their out-of-cage time and be ready to intervene if one bird begins to show aggression toward the other. Separate the birds if they begin fighting with one another by throwing a towel over each one and placing them back in their respective cages.

If the birds don't show signs of being aggressive toward each other, allow them to interact on their own terms and timetable. In time, they should get along, but becoming best friends is not a guarantee, even with the best preparations on your part.

6

The Well-Behaved Macaw

This chapter looks at what can be one of the most enjoyable parts of macaw ownership: taming and training your bird to behave properly. Macaws are extremely intelligent birds, so they should easily learn the basics of behavior, which can leave you time to teach them some amazing tricks.

Training time, when accompanied by proper handling, offers opportunities for you to build a stronger bond with your bird. Having a trained macaw will also allow you to let your bird out of his cage more often, which will make his life more interesting. In order for your bird to be safe when he's out of his cage, he needs to know a few training commands so he will be easy to handle when he's spending out-of-cage time with you and your family.

The most important part of the training process is to make it enjoyable for you and your bird. If you find time to really enjoy your macaw while you're training him, you'll both get more out of the time spent together. Macaws are sensitive to their owners' moods, so your bird is less likely to react well to training if you are tired, angry, or stressed. If you're a happy playmate, on the other hand, your bird will willingly join in the fun!

Why Should I Train My Macaw?

If you doubt the wisdom of training your macaw, consider the havoc an untrained macaw can wreak on your home. He will quickly destroy furniture,

A properly trained macaw is a well-behaved and affectionate pet.

What Your Macaw's Body Language Means

Although your macaw may not have a large verbal vocabulary, he can let you know how he feels by body language and gestures. Listed below are some emotions that could result in your or another family member's being bitten if you don't know what to watch out for:

Aggressiveness: beak clicking, open-mouthed perching, tail fanning, wing drumming, and wings being lifted over the bird's back.

Defensiveness: beak clicking, beak wiping on the perch, foot raising, and an open-mouthed attack posture.

Excitement: eye pinning (pupils rapidly expand, contract, and expand again), feather fluffing, and high activity levels.

Possessiveness: biting a particular person in the home, driving people away from a chosen person or thing, and hissing.

knickknacks, electronic equipment, and almost anything else you value in your home with his powerful beak, which he may also use to nip you if he doesn't know any better.

On the other hand, a trained macaw is an enjoyable pet. He is a handleable, manageable animal that can safely spend time with your family and friends. You can help your bird put some of his excess energy—which he would otherwise use to get into trouble—into learning various tricks.

Training time with your macaw is time for the two of you to be together, which should have been a major factor in your decision to bring your bird into your home. Like any other parrot, your macaw requires regular attention from and interaction with you for his mental health (you and your family are his substitute flock, after all, and members

of a flock spend time together daily), so why not pay attention to your bird by training him?

What Doesn't Work in Macaw Training

You're probably wondering which methods of avian discipline work and which ones don't. We're going to start with a brief discussion of what doesn't work because you may be tempted, in a moment of anger or frustration, to try some of these ineffective methods.

- Dropping bird to the ground
- Putting the bird in a dark room
- Spraying the bird with water
- Shouting at the bird
- Striking the bird
- Throwing things at him

All of these methods were probably tried by parrot owners in the old days of training and taming wild-

A macaw may blush when excited—the bare skin on his face will become red or pink.

caught birds, and not one of them was very effective. Instead, all were cruel attempts to control an intelligent creature by force and intimidation. No matter how frustrated you get with your macaw, do not resort to these methods. Parrots do not respond well to these training methods–they can in fact be highly counterproductive– but they do respond well to another type of training: positive reinforcement.

Positive Reinforcement Works

Macaws, like all other parrots, respond very well to positive reinforcement–it's probably the best way to train a parrot, in fact! Use positive reinforcement throughout your training sessions to help your bird enjoy them even more. Provide a combination of verbal and non-verbal praise as a reward for appropriate behavior, but don't rely too heavily on food treats as your sole method of behavioral reward. You can also use cuddling, scratching a favorite tickle spot, or even one-on-one playtime as rewards for your bird's correct behavior. You'll have to find out which rewards work best with your macaw and then use a combination of them to recognize him for his hard work.

Remember to praise your macaw for good behavior as soon as you see him behaving as you want him to. Many of us bird owners forget to praise and reward our pets when they behave well, but they need these little boosters to remind them how they are expected to behave. Tell your macaw he's being good when he plays quietly, because you will both reward and reinforce the behavior with your words.

Macaw Basic Training

Without trust between you and your macaw, training will go nowhere. It will be a frustrating, useless exercise, so begin your training by developing your bird's trust.

Forging Trust

A good first step in developing trust is to allow your macaw ample time to feel comfortable in your home. He will need at least a week or two to feel comfortable in your home after arriving from the breeder or bird specialty store, so don't begin your first training session for several weeks after your bird becomes part of your home (although you should talk to him, spend time near his cage, offer treats, and otherwise get him used to your presence).

Another initial step in trust-building is to speak softly to your bird. Use his name often when you're talking to him so he will become accustomed to the sound of your voice. Sit quietly by his cage for short sessions frequently during the first few days to have him adjust to having you close to him. Leave a small treat in your macaw's food bowl at the end of each of these sessions so that your bird will have a positive association with your being close to him.

To gauge your bird's comfort level in your home, see how he reacts when you enter a room. If he screams, squawks, or tries to fly away when you approach his cage, he isn't comfortable yet. If he comes over to investigate what you are doing, he's ready to begin his training.

Step Up

Start your training sessions in a small room, such as the bathroom. Take your macaw, a short dowel perch, your bird's carrier or travel cage, and some of his favorite treats into the room. Place your macaw's cage on the floor. Make sure the toilet bowl lid and shower stall doors are closed, and then sit down on the floor beside the cage.

Open the cage door and let your macaw come out on his own. Offer a treat just out of your bird's reach so he has to leave the cage to get it. Offer your treat-free hand as a perch and say "Step up" as you hold the treat higher than your bird's head so he has to reach up for it. In reaching up, he may *step up* and you can slide your hand under his foot to reinforce the idea of stepping up. Allow your bird to enjoy the treat before continuing.

Put the perch in front of your macaw after he's out of his cage and repeat the "step up" command as you slide the perch under his foot and gently lift it up. If he steps onto the perch, praise him and raise the perch slowly until it is about mid-chest level. Keep your macaw on the perch for a few minutes, then take him over to his cage and turn the perch so that he

Step up is one basic command you should teach your macaw, and it's a good idea to teach him to step onto your arm and a wooden perch.

How Your Child Can Help Train Your Macaw

If your older children or teenagers have the interest, they may be ideal candidates to be your macaw's trainer. 'Tweens and teens may be inclined to invest time each day in working with your macaw to review what he's learned and teach him new words and tricks.

My stepdaughter Rhonda has a way with animals, from parakeets to chickens and sheep. She began training her parakeet, Andre, to do tricks shortly after she received him as a Christmas present when she was nine. She spent time with Andre each day after school, reviewing what the bird had learned, and offering him verbal praise and kisses when he did well. She also taught him a few words, which he said frequently in his little parakeet voice.

Because of Rhonda's patient, consistent training, Andre learned a variety of tricks. He would drop coins onto a table in front of a chosen person or look both ways before entering the hallway that passed by Rhonda's room so he wouldn't be stepped on.

The secret to Rhonda's training success was simple: she genuinely wanted to spend time with Andre. She knew early on that he was a clever bird and that he seemed to enjoy doing new things. No one asked her to train Andre; it was something she chose to do because she wanted to, and she ended up having a greater relationship with her parakeet because she put the effort into teaching him to do some tricks.

steps off it onto the cage top. Tell him to "Step down" as he gets off the perch. Repeat these two commands once more during this first training session, and reward your macaw with a treat for behaving well.

If your macaw is reluctant to step onto the perch, resist the temptation to chase him around the room with the perch. Take a deep breath, and then talk quietly to your macaw to help him calm down if he seems anxious. Offer him a treat when he seems calm.

Don't let the first training session last more than 15 minutes, regardless of whether your bird steps onto your hand or the perch. Return your macaw to his cage at the end of the session, praise him for being good, and give him a treat. Repeat this training session daily until your macaw confidently steps onto and off the perch

As your bird's confidence increases, alternate between having him *step up* and *step down* onto and off your hand and the perch. Your macaw may occasionally appear to be about to bite you as he steps onto your hand, but he's using his beak to test the strength of the perch. Do not flinch or pull away as your macaw uses his beak to see whether your hand is a suitable perch, because you will be inadvertently teaching your bird to bite. If your macaw learns that you are afraid of his beak, he may start biting you and other family members just to see the reaction he gets from biting, which will not lead to a positive bird-owner relationship.

The *step up* and *step down* commands are the basic commands you will use to control your bird for the rest of his life, so it's important to teach them to your macaw when he's young. If your macaw gets himself into a potentially dangerous situation in your home, knowing the *step up* command can give you a chance to rescue your bird before something bad happens.

Riding in Cars with Macaws

A travel carrier is an important accessory for your macaw. It will provide a safe way for him to travel to the veterinarian's office, and it will also be a convenient temporary shelter during cage-cleaning sessions.

Your macaw will probably explore his travel carrier as soon as you put it together and show it to him, but some birds are less enthusiastic about new things. To help your shy bird adjust to his carrier, there are some things you can do.

Start by placing the assembled carrier near your macaw's regular cage. Give him a few days to see the carrier from a distance, and then gradually move it closer to his cage. Within a

Go slowly and offer rewards to be sure your macaw isn't afraid of being in his carrier or travel cage.

No Shoulder Birds!

While it may look cool when you see a pirate with a macaw on his shoulder in the movies, don't let your bird sit on your shoulder regularly. Your macaw is a large bird with the potential to do serious damage to your eyes, ears, or face if he bites you, even accidentally. Birds on shoulders also are harder to control because you can't see or reach them easily. It may seem convenient to let your macaw ride on your shoulder, but it's actually a bad idea.

week or so, the sight of the carrier shouldn't be disturbing to your macaw. Remove your macaw from his regular cage and put him into his carrier, but don't force him—if he's scared or nervous, put him near the carrier and proceed more slowly. Leave the door open so he can get out of the carrier if he feels stressed. Praise your bird for staying in the carrier, and repeat the exercise several times a day to increase his comfort level.

Once your macaw appears to be comfortable in the carrier with the door open, close the carrier door. Again, offer praise and a reward to your bird for staying in the closed carrier. Open the door immediately if your macaw seems stressed. If the closed door doesn't appear to bother him, see whether he will stay in the carrier for a few minutes and then reward him. Do this several times daily until your macaw seems

comfortable in the carrier.

After your macaw is acclimated to the closed carrier, take bird and carrier to your car and shut the car door. If your macaw seems content in the car, take him for a short ride. If he seems stressed, take the carrier out of the car and reassure him that everything is okay.

Take time to work with your bird each day until he seems comfortable being inside his carrier in your car. Drive your bird around the block to see how he likes car travel. Your macaw will probably enjoy car travel, but some birds are prone to carsickness, so it's best to start training your macaw to enjoy car rides from an early age.

The location of your bird's travel carrier can sometimes resolve carsickness issues. Some birds need to watch the world go by to distract them, while others need to have their carriers covered and positioned lower than the window height so they can't look outside. You'll have to experiment to see which location in your vehicle works best for your bird if he's prone to carsickness. Whether your macaw faces the direction you are traveling or faces the side of the car can also make a difference in carsickness.

Raising a Well-Adjusted Macaw

Some macaw owners may discover as their birds mature that the birds have difficulty entertaining themselves because they've been held and cuddled and fussed over by family members when they were cute little chicks. To help your bird cope with growing up, here are some suggestions.

First, let your young macaw spend time in his cage by himself from Day 1. Many new bird owners want to hold their baby parrot all the time, and the bird becomes confused as the novelty of bird ownership wears off for the human members of the household and they return to their normal routines as the bird begins to grow up.

Show your young macaw his toys and make a little fuss over them so he will take an interest, then give him some time to explore his cage so he will be able to play independently as he grows up. Verbally praise your bird for playing or entertaining himself.

Next, set realistic boundaries for your bird. Don't cater to him exclusively, and don't rush to satisfy every whim. Excess catering sets the stage for disaster because you'll soon have a demanding little feathered tyrant on your hands.

Finally, don't let your macaw climb onto things that put his eye level higher than yours. In the avian world, height equals safety and confidence, so the higher your macaw climbs, the less manageable he may become. It's going to be pretty difficult to get a macaw down off a curtain rod at ceiling height, for example, but if you control your macaw so that he doesn't climb that high, he will be easier to handle. Also, by using positive training methods, your macaw will prefer being with you to being on the curtain rod.

Trick-Training Macaws

If you want to build on the trust you and your macaw share, begin teaching him to do tricks. Whenever possible, create a trick that uses a behavior your bird does naturally and turn it into a trick. If your macaw picks up one foot frequently, he's a good candidate to learn to wave or to shake hands. If he readily picks things up with his beak, he can learn to drop coins into a bank.

To trick-train your macaw, set up a quiet place in your home where he can learn without distractions. Set up a perch or T-stand on which he can sit, and have some of his favorite treats available to use as rewards. In addition to the food treats, praise your macaw when he's successful at doing his new

With patience and positive reinforcement, your macaw can learn lots of fun tricks.

trick, because you'll eventually use praise instead of food rewards to get him to perform his tricks.

Let's look at a simple trick–waving–and a more complicated trick–fetching–to see how you can teach them to your macaw.

Waving

To teach your bird to wave, hold up a pencil, chopstick, or something similar so your bird can reach for it with one of his feet. Have the pencil just out of reach and cue your bird with the word "wave." Praise your macaw when he reaches for the pencil, even if he makes only a small move toward it at first. Repeat the process each day until your bird seems to associate "wave" with reaching for the pencil. Continue to polish your bird's skills by eliminating the pencil and instead using only the verbal cue. Reward and praise your pet when he raises his foot.

Fetching

To teach your bird to fetch, you'll need to teach him the parts of the trick so he can learn the steps, then put them together to perform the trick.

A good first step in teaching your macaw to fetch is to teach him to drop an item on command so it's available to be thrown and fetched. Let your macaw play with the item to be fetched and say, "Drop!" when he drops it on his own. Praise and repeat until your bird seems to link the cue and the action.

Next, place the item to be fetched a short distance from your macaw and cue him with "Get it!" (or another appropriate verbal cue). Praise your bird when he runs after the item, and repeat this part of the training until your macaw seems to associate the cue with running after the item. Keep moving the item a little farther. Then start throwing the item instead of just placing it.

Finally, teach your macaw to retrieve the item. Throw the item and have your bird chase after it. When he picks up the item, cue him with "Bring it here!" and meet him as he returns to you. Praise the bird for fetching the item, then repeat the process, eliminating the part where you meet him as he returns to you after a few tries. Praise and repeat until he perfects the trick.

Take time to create unusual tricks for you and your macaw to

Catalina macaw waving "hello." This is a fairly easy trick that most macaws can learn quickly.

perform. You'll enjoy teaching your bird these special tricks, and your bird will have fun learning something new.

Mixing Macaws with Other Pets

You'll need to properly socialize your macaw to other members of your household (human and non-human) to ensure everyone's safety. Human family members need to know how to hold and handle your macaw, and your macaw needs to be supervised in his interactions with other family pets because he could accidentally harm one of them, or they could hurt him. Here are some things to keep in mind when your macaw mixes with other pets in your home.

Other Birds

Another bird in your home may be in danger from your macaw's large and powerful beak, depending on the other bird's size. Canaries, finches, budgies, cockatiels, and lovebirds should not be allowed to play with your macaw; the size difference between the two birds makes mixing them inadvisable. Interactions between macaws and medium-size parrots, such as Amazons or African greys, should be closely monitored to protect the smaller birds' safety. Even playtime between two macaws or a macaw and a cockatoo needs to be supervised because there's still the potential for a serious bite injury.

Cats and Dogs

A cat in your home may consider your macaw a toy until the bird bites the

Clicker Training

You may find using a clicker to be an effective aid to trick-training your parrot. The clicking noise serves as a bridge between the bird's good behavior and an impending treat, and many birds find it to be a pleasant sound.

To train your macaw with a clicker, use the clicker first along with a treat to reward your macaw's good behavior. The critical part is to click exactly when your bird performs the behavior you want. Click and feed your bird so he associates the sound with the reward. As your bird becomes more accustomed to the sound of the clicker, begin to decrease the food rewards and reinforce your macaw's behavior using just the clicker.

cat, but your macaw could be clawed or bitten if your cat attempts to chase it. Animal bites, especially from cats, are potentially deadly to your macaw without prompt veterinary care.

Depending on its size and breed, a dog may make a good companion for a macaw. Smaller dogs will probably steer clear of your macaw's beak, but medium to large dogs will likely form a peaceful alliance with your bird. If your dog is a sighthound, he may instinctively try to hunt your macaw. Always supervise all interactions between your dog and your bird. Even if your dog doesn't mean to harm your macaw—or vice versa—overenthusiastic play can result in serious injuries.

Other Pets

Pocket pets, such as hamsters and gerbils, would likely be in danger of being seriously injured by your macaw's beak, so interaction between these two types of pets is not recommended.

Reptile pets are probably not a good mix with your macaw, because many of them will likely view your bird as a snack or meal. Conversely, small reptiles and amphibians are preyed on by birds, so encounters with your macaw will stress them out (at best).

Introducing Your Macaw and Your Children

With proper education and training, macaws and children should get along

Macaws can get overexcited when they play together, so you will need to supervise your birds at all times.

well. Macaws are sturdy enough to withstand handling by children, but the children may be intimidated by the macaw's size and its large beak. Your macaw may also make loud noises that may or may not frighten your children, but your children's boisterous play may startle your macaw until he becomes accustomed to it and joins in the fun.

You can help your children build a good relationship with your macaw by providing consistent guidance. Let them know that the bird sometimes needs time alone in his cage to play quietly and that he may not feel like playing with them all the time. Also explain to them that there will be times during the day that your macaw will take naps, just as they did when they were younger. Show them how to hold and handle your macaw, and oversee all interactions to prevent your children from being bitten and your macaw from being injured by accidental mishandling.

Will My Macaw Talk?

Many bird owners hope that they will be lucky enough to have a talking bird, and while most parrots have the ability to talk, some species are better talkers than others. The species with the greatest potential to talk are the African grey, the budgie, the Quaker parakeet, and some of the Amazon parrots.

Macaws are not well known for their talking ability, but your bird may learn a few words or phrases. Here are the steps to follow to teach your bird to talk.

Start teaching your bird to talk when he's young because younger birds are more likely to learn to speak than older birds.

Keep a talking bird as a single pet because birds kept in pairs are more likely to speak "bird" than to use human language. If a bird has another bird to bond with, he will communicate with that bird in a common language. If he's kept as part of a human flock, he is more likely to speak in our language to communicate with us. Similarly, eliminate mirrored toys from your bird's cage because he will try to bond with the avian reflection in the mirror, speaking "bird" to it instead of using language to talk to you.

Set up a quiet training area to reduce distractions. Consider how difficult it is to have a conversation in your home when your children are all talking, your spouse is asking you a question, the phone is ringing, and the television is on. Your macaw will have an equally difficult time learning his speech lessons if you're trying to teach him something when background distractions are occurring. Your bird may also be eager to please you because he's receiving one-on-one attention, and distractions will detract from his focus.

Select a single phrase and stay with it because repetition offers your macaw the best chance of learning the phrase successfully. Build on the basics once your bird has learned a few phrases to expand his vocabulary.

Enunciate so that your bird can hear what you are saying clearly and repeat it with equal clarity. Mumbling owners lead to mumbling birds, so be sure to speak clearly.

Use the chosen phrase in context to make training easier. If you say "Hello" to your bird each time you enter his room, he will come to associate the word with the act of entering a room or seeing someone for the first time. Phrases used in context are more likely to be used often in conversation, which makes teaching them easier. Often-used phrases are more likely to be used by your macaw, too.

Keep training sessions short to make the most of your macaw's attention span. Plan on teaching your bird in 15-minute blocks because that's about as long as he can focus.

Conclude your training sessions on a positive note to keep your macaw interested. If a session isn't going well, come back to it another time. Your macaw will pick up on anger or frustration from you if a session doesn't go as you had planned, so it's best to try the session at a different time when you are both in a better frame of mind.

A little patience goes a long way when teaching a bird to talk. This goes along with the idea of ending on a positive note, and it really does help to be a patient teacher. Smile frequently during the training sessions and enjoy them. If you're having fun, chances are your macaw will too, which will produce better results for both of you.

Take time to listen to your bird, especially as he settles down for bed. Listening may seem like an odd thing to discuss in a section about talking, but you can gauge how the training is going by taking the time to listen to your bird at bedtime. Many parrots test their vocabularies as they fall asleep,

The severe macaw has a reputation for being one of the best talkers of all macaws, but there is no guarantee any parrot will talk.

so you may hear your bird muttering to himself or practicing new words and phrases at that time.

A question that many new bird owners have is whether or not the talking CDs available at pet supply stores or online are effective in teaching a bird to talk. Some birds learn some phrases from the discs, but many tune them out. One-on-one training sessions between you and your bird are the best opportunity for your macaw to learn to talk.

Identifying and Solving Problem Behaviors

Macaws can be prone to five major behavior problems—aggression, biting, chewing, feather picking, and screaming. We'll look briefly at the possible causes and some solutions for each.

Aggression

The most common cause of aggression in adult macaws and other parrots is displaced breeding behavior. The bird is frustrated because he or she can't mate with a chosen human companion, and the bird begins to act aggressively toward that human companion. Signs can include shredding of papers or toys, frequent regurgitation to the chosen companion, and eye pinning (the bird's pupils expand and contract in rapid succession).

Aggression can also be a major reason behind biting, which we'll discuss further in a moment. Aggressive biting can be directed at the chosen human companion, and it's usually confined to facial areas. The macaw is trying to "chase" you away from the rest of your family, and if he's allowed to sit on your shoulder regularly, he will bite at your face because he may perceive the rest of your body as a specialized tree on which you both roost. Or aggressive biting may be directed toward other family members as a way of keeping them away from you and showing them that your bird thinks he's boss.

To reduce the chance of having your bird become an aggressive biter, have all members take turns caring for the macaw when he first joins your home. Have one or two people prepare his food and change his bowls each day, and take turns cleaning his cage each day. Have all family members play with the macaw, and allow all interested family members to take part in his training.

If your bird comes to depend on just one person for his daily care, he may start to pair-bond with that person as he would with an avian mate. If he forms a bond with some or all human family members, he will be less likely to identify one of you as his chosen mate and become aggressive toward you.

Biting
A biting macaw is no fun to handle and usually results in the bird's being left in his cage for longer and longer

Getting Professional Help

If you adopt an adult macaw, you may discover that he has some long-standing behavior problems even after he's adapted to life in your home. Some of them can be overcome with patient retraining, but others may require professional assistance to resolve.

Discuss your macaw's behavior problems with your avian veterinarian. He or she may be able to recommend an avian behaviorist who can help you. Some avian veterinarians have behaviorists on staff at their clinics, while others make referrals to outside professionals. You are especially likely to need a professional behaviorist to help solve a feather-plucking problem.

periods of time. This results in a condition called being cagebound, and it can set up a series of related behavior problems, including screaming and feather plucking.

A macaw may bite because he's afraid, under stress, or feeling a need to breed. Perhaps the most common way a bird becomes a biter is when a young bird uses his beak to explore his surroundings and test the strength of potential perches (including human hands). In the course of his explorations, he may accidentally bite a bit too hard on one of those hand perches, which causes the owner of the bitten hand to scream and pull away. If this sequence continues, the macaw may quickly learn to bite to get the reaction he enjoys (the drama of the screaming person and the hand pulling away).

You can solve a biting problem in your macaw by not showing a strong reaction to accidental bites from young birds. You may also need to regain your bird's trust or give him more supervised out-of-cage time to prevent him from becoming cagebound. Additionally, by rewarding behaviors you want and not rewarding behaviors you don't want (like biting), you encourage your bird to keep from biting you.

Chewing

Macaws are going to chew things to keep their large beaks in condition and to give themselves something to do, so it's up to you to provide appropriate and safe toys on which your bird can chew. Offer your macaw a variety of chew toys from the pet supply store, and supplement them with safe items found around your house, such as empty paper towel rolls, clean cardboard boxes, and nuts in the shell. Supervise your bird closely when he is out of the cage to keep him from chewing on stuff you don't want him chewing on.

Feather Plucking

If your macaw suddenly starts pulling out his feathers, a number of factors could be behind his sudden baldness. He could have an undiagnosed illness, he could be stressed, he could be bored, or he could want to breed. The first step to solving this issue is to take him to your vet to rule out a health problem. If your macaw is physically healthy, the plucking is likely behavioral and can be tricky to solve.

A sometimes-overlooked cause of feather plucking is the use of feather-conditioning products. Although many birds can use these products without incident, some birds feel the need to over-preen their feathers after these products are applied. For your bird's health and well-being, use only clear

This macaw is exhibiting signs of aggression: raised nape feathers and pinning eyes.

warm water on your bird's feathers. You can mist him daily to encourage him to preen normally.

To help alleviate boredom in your macaw, be sure to rotate the toys in his cage regularly. Give your macaw plenty of out-of-cage time and hands-on attention. If the problem continues, you may need to consult an avian behavioral consultant.

Screaming

A macaw may scream for a number of reasons: stress, boredom, isolation, or an unfulfilled desire to mate, among others. In some cases, macaws learn to scream because they were rewarded (in their minds) for past screaming behavior. Macaws love drama, so when you run into a room and make a scene by yelling or shaking your fist at the bird, he loves it and wants to see more of it, so he may scream again.

Rather than screaming, train yourself to simply ask the bird what the problem is. Go into the bird's room and check for dangers or hazards, resolve any problems, then reassure the bird quietly that nothing is wrong. Gently encourage him to play to distract him from screaming, and then leave the room. If he screams again a short time later, calmly reassure him that all is well and remind him again to play. In a short time, your bird should lose interest in screaming for attention, particularly if you remember to give him praise and reinforcement for good behavior.

An unsupervised macaw is likely to chew on things you don't want him to, such as valuable furniture.

Other ways to solve the screaming problem are to reduce the bird's stress level, providing a wider variety of toys to decrease boredom, or moving his cage to a more active part of your home where he can feel a part of daily activities. Rewarding quieter sounds with a treat and ignoring screams also helps a lot in preventing screaming from becoming a habit.

Resources

Organizations

American Federation of Aviculture
P.O.Box 7312
N. Kansas City, MO 64116
Telephone: (816) 421-3214
Fax: (816)421-3214
E-mail: afaoffice@aol.com
www.afabirds.org

Avicultural Society of America
PO Box 5516
Riverside, CA 92517-5516
Telephone: (951) 780-4102
Fax: (951) 789-9366
E-mail: info@asabirds.org
www.asabirds.org

Aviculture Society of the United
Kingdom
Arcadia-The Mounts-East Allington-
Totnes
Devon TQ9 7QJ
United Kingdom
E-mail: admin@avisoc.co.uk
www.avisoc.co.uk/

The Gabriel Foundation
1025 Acoma Street
Denver, CO 80204
Telephone: (970) 963-2620
Fax: (970) 963-2218
E-mail: gabriel@thegabrielfoundation.org
www.thegabrielfoundation.org

International Association of Avian
Trainers and Educators
350 St. Andrews Fairway

Memphis, TN 38111
Telephone: (901) 685-9122
Fax: (901) 685-7233
E-mail: secretary@iaate.org
www.iaate.org

The Parrot Society of Australia
P.O. Box 75
Salisbury, Queensland 4107
Australia
E-mail: petbird@parrotsociety.org.au
http: //www.partosociety.org.au

Emergency Resources and Rescue Organizations

ASPCA Animal Poison Control Center
Telephone: (888) 426-4435
E-mail: napcc@aspca.org (for non-
emergency, general information only)
www.apcc.aspca.org

Bird Hotline
P.O. Box 1411
Sedona, AZ 86339-1411
E-mail: birdhotline@birdhotline.com
www.birdhotline.com/

Bird Placement Program
P.O. Box 347392
Parma, OH 44134
Telephone: (330) 722-1627
E-mail: birdrescue5@hotmail.com
www.birdrescue.com

Parrot Rehabilitation Society
P.O. Box 620213
San Diego, CA 92102
Telephone: (619) 224-6712
E-mail: prsorg@yahoo.com
www.parrotsociety.org

Petfinder
www.petfinder.com

Veterinary Resources

Association of Avian Veterinarians
P.O.Box 811720
Boca Raton, FL 33481-1720
Telephone: (561) 393-8901
Fax: (561) 393-8902
E-mail: AAVCTRLOFC@aol.com
www.aav.org

Exotic Pet Vet.Net
www.exoticpetvet.net

Internet Resources

AvianWeb
www.avianweb.com/

BirdCLICK
www.geocities.com/Heartland/
Acres/9154/

HolisticBird.org
www.holisticbird.org

The Parrot Pages
www.parrotpages.com

Parrot Parrot
www.parrotparrot.com/

The Tambopata Macaw Project
www.macawproject.org

Magazines

Bird Talk
3 Burroughs
Irvine, CA 92618
Telephone: 949-855-8822
Fax: (949) 855-3045
www.birdtalkmagazine.com

Good Bird
PO Box 684394
Austin, TX 78768
Telephone: 512-423-7734
Fax: (512) 236-0531
E-mail: info@goodbirdinc.com
www.goodbirdinc.com

Books

Deutsch, Robin. *Good Parrotkeeping.*
TFH Publications, Inc.

Deutsch, Robin. *The Click That Does the Trick.* TFH Publications, Inc.

Deutsch, Robin. *The Healthy Bird Cookbook.* TFH Publications, Inc.

Heidenreich, Barbara. *The Parrot Problem Solver.* TFH Publications, Inc.

Moutsaki, Nikki. *Your Outta Control Bird.* TFH Publications, Inc.

O'Connor, Rebecca K. *A Parrot for Life.*
TFH Publications, Inc.

Rach, Julie. *The Simple Guide to Bird Care and Training.* TFH Publications, Inc. caring concerns, 24
as family members, 20

Index

Boldfaced numbers indicate illustrations.

medications for, **73**, 74, 79
multi-birds issues, 86–87, **87**
obesity, 53, 80–82, **82**
older macaws, care of, 85–86, **86**
pasteurellosis, 76
PDDS, 82–83
physical exams, 73–74
poisoning, 77–78
polyomavirus, 82, **83**
psittacine circovirus 1, 83
psittacosis, 83–84
pulmonary hypersensitivity syndrome, 84
seizures, 78
stress, 81
tests, 74
veterinarian office visits, **72**, 73
vitamin A deficiency, 84–85, **85**
heatstroke, 77
history of macaws in the Americas, 6
home safety concerns, 38
home-cooked treats, 51
homemade bird toys, 34
hyacinth macaws (*Anodorhynchus hyacinthinus*), **7**, 8, 13, 17
hybrid macaws, 14

I
identification, microchip, 67
Illiger's macaws (*Primolius maracana*), 8, 15, **16**, 17
illness. *See also* health issues
    parrot specific, 78–85
    signs of, 75, **76**
infections, 80
insurance for pets, 74

K
kitchen safety concerns, 38

L
lifespan of macaws, 17
linings for cages, 29–30
living room safety concerns, 38
locating
    avian veterinarians, 71–73
    macaws, 19–21

M
macaw wasting disease, 82
manzanita perches, 31
medications, **73**, 74, 79
microchip identification, 67
military macaws (*Ara militaris*), 8, 13–14, **13**, 17
mineral licks, 43
minerals in diet, 43–44
miniature macaws, 11, 14–17

mirrored toys, 101
modern uses of macaws, 6–7
mold in peanuts, 50
molting, 65–66
multi-bird issues, 73, 86–87, **87**, 99, 101
Munn, Charles, 43

N
nail care, 60–62, **61–62**
natural environment
    diet in, 42–43, **42**, **100**
    living conditions in, 9–11, **9**
noble macaws, 15, **18**
nonstick cookware concerns, 38, 84
nuts in diet, 50, **51**

O
obesity, 53, 80–82, **82**
office visits, veterinarian, 73–75
older macaws, 48, 85–86, **86**
organic diets, 47, 50
ornithosis, 83
other pets and macaws, 99–100
out-of-cage time, 19
overheating concerns, 26, 77

P
palm nuts, 42
papovavirus, 82
parrot fever, 83
parrot rescue groups, 21
pasteurellosis, 76
PBFDS (psittacine beak and feather disease syndrome), 83
PDDS (proventricular dilation disease syndrome), 82–83
pelleted diet foods, 46
people food, feeding, 51–52
perches, 30–32, **30–32**
pet qualities, 16–19
physical exams, 73–74
placement
    of cages, 28–29
    of perches, 32
playgyms, 35–36, **37**
poisoning, 77–78
polyomavirus, 82, **83**
possessiveness, body language showing, 91
preening, **57–58**, 58
Primolius auricollis (yellow-collared macaws), 8, 16–17, **21**
Primolius maracana (Illiger's macaws), 8, **16**, 17
private breeders, 20–21
proteins in diet, 43
proventricular dilation disease syndrome

Dedication

For mi famiglia Mancini: Ron, Randy, Debbie, Richie, Michele, Rhonda, Salvatore, Michael, Joseph, and Rose (and the Sampsons, Teufels, Sandovals, Vindells, Klyverts, Repoles, Wislohs, and Brocks)

About the Author

Birds have attracted Julie Mancini's attention for most of her life, beginning with pigeons her father fed to entertain her when she was a toddler. She shared her home with a parakeet and a special-needs African grey parrot for many years. Now, Julie and her family keep a small flock of laying hens and a herd of goats on their Iowa acreage. Julie has been a freelance writer for 15 years. She has written 20 books and numerous articles on companion animal care.

Photo Credits